W9-ACJ-767

ONE COUNTRY

ONE COUNTRY

A Bold Proposal to End
the Israeli-Palestinian Impasse

ALI ABUNIMAH

Metropolitan Books
Henry Holt and Company
NEW YORK

Metropolitan Books
Henry Holt and Company, LLC
Publishers since 1866
175 Fifth Avenue
New York, New York 10010

Metropolitan Books ® and ® are registered
trademarks of Henry Holt and Company, LLC.

Library of Congress Cataloging-in-Publication data

Abunimah, Ali.
   One country : a bold proposal to end the Israeli-Palestinian impasse / by Ali
Abunimah.—1st ed.
      p.   cm.
   Includes index.
   ISBN-13: 978-0-8050-8034-6
   ISBN-10: 0-8050-8034-1
   1. Arab-Israeli conflict—1933— —Peace.   I. Title.
DS119.76.A355 2006
956.9405'4—dc22   2006043849

Henry Holt books are available for special promotions and
premiums. For details contact: Director, Special Markets.

First Edition 2006

Designed by Adam B. Bohannon

Printed in the United States of America
10 9   8   7   6   5   4   3   2   1

For Usama Hussein Abu al-Sheikh, and for all the people of Shatila. Your strength and humanity remain my inspiration.

CONTENTS

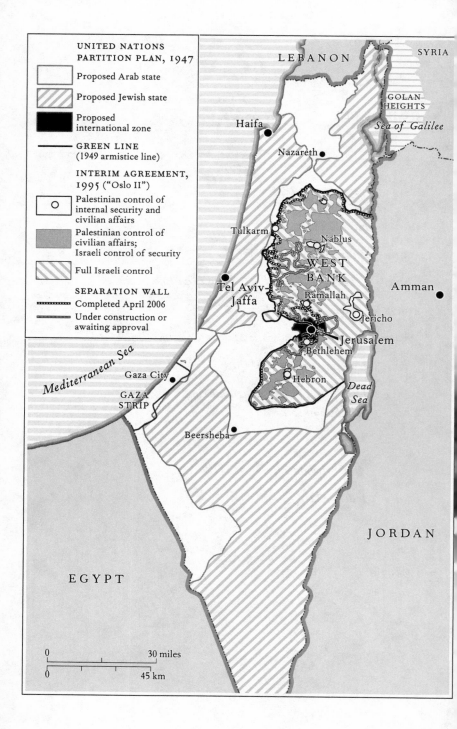

UNITED NATIONS
PARTITION PLAN, 1947

Proposed Arab state

Proposed Jewish state

Proposed
international zone

GREEN LINE
(1949 armistice line)

INTERIM AGREEMENT,
1995 ("Oslo II")

Palestinian control of
internal security and
civilian affairs

Palestinian control of
civilian affairs;
Israeli control of security

Full Israeli control

SEPARATION WALL
Completed April 2006
Under construction or
awaiting approval

LEBANON   SYRIA

GOLAN
HEIGHTS

Sea of Galilee

Haifa

Nazareth

Tulkarm   Nablus

WEST
BANK

Tel Aviv-   Ramallah   Amman
Jaffa

Jericho

Jerusalem

Bethlehem

Mediterranean Sea

Gaza City   Hebron

GAZA   Dead
STRIP   Sea

Beersheba

JORDAN

EGYPT

0   30 miles

0   45 km

ONE COUNTRY

Introduction

What will it take to make peace between Israelis and Palestinians? Some say we must forget the past. I think we have to start by remembering it. My first memory of Palestine is from a supermarket in London. Before I was old enough to go to school, I remember regularly accompanying my mother to the Safeway in Ealing Broadway. One day we were buying oranges and I pointed at some big, beautiful-looking ones. "No, not those," my mother said, "they are from Jaffa, they are our oranges." This made no sense to my five-year-old mind. If they were our oranges, why couldn't we have them? My mother explained to me that the citrus groves of Jaffa belonged to Palestinians, to people like us, until the Israelis took them over.

My maternal grandfather, Ali Najjar, was a wealthy man who had inherited land from his father, and acquired more along the way, buying up whatever his brothers wanted to sell. My mother's family came from the village of Lifta, whose sturdy stone houses with their gentle, arched windows were built on steep hillsides just northwest of Jerusalem. The village's history is documented from before Roman times, and in the early twentieth century, as the population grew, houses crept up the hill until they touched the Jerusalem neighborhood of Rumayma.[1] It was here that my grandfather built a splendid new house overlooking the valley below, which is where my mother was born in 1939. Recalling it today, she describes six spacious bedrooms, separate dining and living rooms. It was the house of a prosperous family, whose furniture included a piano. It was near a forest, and surrounded by a large garden with fruit trees and every variety of flower. My mother remembers most vividly a red climbing rose, which scaled the height of the wall, and now she explains to me that this is why she planted a climbing rose bush in front of our house in Amman. Her father also had a fine car, a Chevrolet, and a driver who sometimes took her and her sisters to school.

On Jaffa Street, at that time the bustling heart of modern Jerusalem, my grandfather built an imposing building, said to be the first in the area with the advanced convenience of central heating. Many of his tenants were doctors, principally German Jews. My mother recalls regularly visiting one of the tenants, a Dr. Hirsh, who treated her as a child. "He was a very kind man," she remembers. "He was an old man, not a young doctor." On Jewish holidays my grandparents would send food to Dr. Hirsh, and during Passover, he would send my mother's family matzoh, the unleavened bread that in Jewish tradition symbolizes the flight from Egypt. "I liked it," she says, and I finally understand why throughout my own childhood in London and Brussels whenever matzoh would appear in the stores around Passover, she would buy it and we would eat it at home.

One of my mother's strongest childhood memories was of a

little girl called Miriam, the daughter of a Jewish furrier and his wife who rented the apartment on the first floor of my grandfather's house. "They were very nice days," my mother says. "We would come home from school, have lunch, and then go down and play with the neighbors. We played with this little girl all the time. We loved her. And my father loved her too. I wish I knew what happened to her." Miriam had also been born in my grandfather's house.

That happy, comfortable childhood in Rumayma came to an end in early 1948. For my mother, too young to be fully aware of the swirling politics of the Palestine conflict, the change was unexpected. All of a sudden, she started to see guns. "One day we were sleeping," she recalls, "and we heard gunshots and we ran out to see what was happening. . . . We were scared and we were crying and I remember my father and my brother carrying guns and shooting from the veranda." Lifta, Rumayma, and the adjacent districts of Sheikh Badr were among the first communities that Palestinians left. According to Israeli historian Benny Morris, "Hostilities there were triggered when the Haganah (the main Jewish militia) killed the owner, who came from the nearby Arab village of Qalunya, of a petrol station in the mixed neighborhood of Romema (Rumayma); they had suspected him of informing Arab irregulars about the departure of Jewish convoys to Tel Aviv." Qalunya villagers retaliated the next day by throwing a grenade at a Jewish bus. On December 28, 1947, the Stern Gang, a militia led by future Israeli prime minister Yitzhak Shamir, attacked a coffeehouse in Lifta, spraying it with machine-gun fire and killing, according to the *New York Times,* five patrons.[2] Daily exchanges of fire ensued, and the Haganah and other Jewish militias repeatedly attacked until the raids, "as was their intention, caused the evacuation of the Arabs of Lifta and Romema during December 1947 and January 1948."[3]

My mother remembers the day she left Lifta and how my grandfather calmed his daughters: "Why are you crying? Why should you take anything with you? We are coming back in a few days. It will all be finished." So my grandmother packed only a few clothes and towels for the children, covered the furniture with sheets, and locked the door. My grandfather, grandmother, their daughters—Arifa, Rif'a, Nahida, Aida, my mother, Samira, Nawal, and Naila—their brother, Arif, his wife, Salwa, and the couple's baby girl, Orayb, mounted the back of a rented truck and trundled off, never to return. Their first refuge was the home of family friends in the Bak'a area of southern Jerusalem, until a few months later when the fighting reached them there and along with the rest of the population they fled. My grandfather took his family to Jordan, where most of his descendants still live. My mother recalls the first harsh days of their exile, living in a house made of mud in the village of Sweileh, with none of the modern conveniences of running water and indoor toilets they had been accustomed to in Palestine. Despite the loss of the family home and much of his land, my grandfather still had money in the bank and was able to reestablish himself. But many among the wealthier Palestinians were far less fortunate, losing all their property and even their bank accounts. And for hundreds of thousands of villagers all their wealth consisted of the land and homes they had been forced to leave for teeming refugee camps in Lebanon, Syria, Jordan, Gaza, and the West Bank.

This is how the calamity of the Palestinians, *al-Nakba*, began for my family. David Ben-Gurion, the leader of the Yishuv—the pre-state Zionist establishment in Palestine—saw what happened in Jerusalem through completely different eyes. On February 7, 1948, he told the leaders of his party, "From your entry into Jerusalem through Lifta-Romema, through Mahane Yehuda, King George Street and Mea Shearim—there are no strangers [i.e., Arabs]. One hundred per cent Jews. Since Jerusalem's destruction in the days of the Romans—it hasn't been so Jewish as it is now. In many Arab districts in the west—one sees not one Arab. I do not assume this will change." He added, "What happened in Jerusalem . . . could well happen in great parts of the country."[4] So it was that my mother, the "stranger," was gone from the home where she was born, and in her place and that of three-quarters of the Palestinian population dispersed in those terrible days, the State of Israel arose.

What is there in these fragments of memory? How should I interpret them? Are they evidence of a harmonious past that could have become a harmonious future but for a few fateful decisions? Were they no more than rare instances in a sea of hostility and fear? I find these recollections compelling. There was a time when ordinary, banal contacts occurred between people, and then at a certain moment they stopped. Were people who worked together, played together, exchanged gifts, and helped each other destined to be enemies? Perhaps the warm relationships between my mother's family and their Jewish neighbors were rare. No doubt there was plenty of tension.

My father's childhood was different, yet he too recalls warm relations with Jews in Palestine. He grew up in Battir, a village near Bethlehem. The *fallahin,* the villagers, would meet Jews coming to visit ruins up on the hill above Battir, which the villagers themselves called *khirbet al-yahud* (the Jews' ruins). But as fear and mistrust of Zionist intentions in Palestine grew, so did hostility to these visits; in Jewish nationalist mythology, Battir was once the site of Beitar, the last Jewish town to fall to the Romans in their effort to crush the revolt led by Shimon Bar-Kochba. It wasn't until 1990 that the fears of the villagers triggered by the Jewish visitors decades earlier were realized. Today, "Beitar" is the name of a West Bank settlement of thirty thousand Israelis built on nearby lands confiscated from Palestinians. On the settlement's Web site, under the title "Ancient Beitar," is an image of modern Battir, my father's village, with the caption, "remains of the Beitar fortress," as if the Palestinian homes and village mosque clearly visible in the picture simply didn't exist. Battir today, along with neighboring villages, is being walled in, their cultivable lands annexed and taken by the settlers, and their people isolated and imprisoned in a ghetto. Yet even amid the memories of a creeping conflict, my father remembers more neighborly encounters. On several occasions, the celebrated Jewish ophthalmologist, Dr. Avraham Ticho, came to visit the family home and treat people in the village. And there were ordinary friendships with Palestinian Jews, many of whom lived simple rural lives that resembled my father's and his family's.

In the clash between Zionism and Palestinian nationalism the fabric of social relations among the country's peoples stood little chance of remaining intact, and many have now given in to the belief that the harmony never existed, or that it can never be restored. But the verdict of conflict without end is predicated in part on what we have chosen to remember and what we prefer to forget. One of the most notorious incidents in the long bloody history was the murder of sixty-seven Jews by an Arab mob in Hebron in 1929. The memory of this massacre, one of Israel's foundation myths, is considered a signal lesson in Arab-Jewish relations and has recently been used by right-wing Zionists to justify the aggressive settlement movement in Hebron along with all of the measures imposed on that city's Palestinian population. But as the Jews of Hebron testified in 1929, most of the city's Jewish community were saved because Muslim neighbors protected them in their own homes and tended to the wounded.[5] How would history look today had that been the signal lesson of the event, had that been the version of history young Israelis were taught? (It is worth noting that many descendants of those Hebron Jews have been vocal in their rejection of the way that today's Jewish settlers have hijacked their history.)[6]

Some might read these words as an indictment of Israel, others as a vindication of a pro-Palestinian stance, but I intend them as neither. Some might say that dwelling on history means I have no desire for reconciliation. Some will simply deny the truth of this history, or say that whatever happened to the Palestinians was justified by their own aggressive provocations or by some greater claim to the country. These are all familiar reactions whenever Palestinians try to tell their story. The question of how the Palestinians came to be in exile has always been at the center of any argument over the legitimacy of Israel. To Israelis and most Jews, the Jewish State is a miracle that represents redemption from the unspeakable horrors of the Nazi Holocaust. Israel is an emotional insurance policy against the visceral vulnerability that many Jews still feel, a vulnerability born of centuries of persecution in Europe. Israel is a touchstone of identity and a rallying point for community. The notion that its creation was achieved with the blood and suffering of others, that bad deeds were done and continue to be done, is unbearable emotionally and threatening politically. *It can't have been*, they say, *therefore, it wasn't*. To Palestinians and most of the Arab world, the creation of the Jewish state meant, first and foremost, the destruction of Palestine.

It seems a commonplace that whoever wins the battle of the past wins the battle of the present. Thus efforts at Israeli-Palestinian dialogue often argue that there must be an "agreed narrative" of the past before we can move toward peace. But any such effort in the current context will produce a false version of history tailored to suit a political purpose, usually the agenda of those with the greatest power. Consequently, Israel exhorts Jews to remember their past while Palestinians are castigated for not forgetting that they are refugees, and that they came to be so because they had no place in the Jewish state created by the Zionist movement.

Peace cannot require Palestinians to acquiesce to the denial of what was done to them. Neither can it require Israeli Jews to view their own presence in Palestine as illegitimate or to change their belief in their right to live there because of ancient historical and spiritual ties. Peace, rather, must be based on how we act toward each other now. It is unacceptable for a Palestinian to draw on his history of oppression and suffering to justify harming innocent Israeli civilians. It is equally unacceptable for an Israeli to invoke his belief in an ancient covenant between God and Abraham to justify bulldozing the home and seizing the land of a Palestinian farmer.

The 1998 Good Friday Agreement, which proposes a political framework for a resolution to the conflict in Ireland, and which was overwhelmingly endorsed in referendums, sets out two principles from which Palestinians and Israelis could learn. First "[i]t is recognized that victims have a right to remember as well as to contribute to a changed society." Second, whatever political arrangements are freely and democratically chosen for the governance of Northern Ireland, the power of the government "shall be exercised with rigorous impartiality on behalf of all the people in the diversity of their identities and traditions and shall be founded on the principles of full respect for, and equality of civil, political, social, and cultural rights, of freedom from discrimination for all citizens, and of parity of esteem and of just and equal treatment for the identity, ethos, and aspirations of both communities." Northern Ireland is still a long way from achieving this ideal, but life has vastly improved since the worst days of "the Troubles" and it is a paradise on earth compared to Palestine/Israel.

The principles of the Good Friday Agreement strike me as particularly powerful. Changing society does not require us to forget or revise the past, and living together does not require us to abandon our identity, culture, and history, even in the context of a bitter and bloody ethnic conflict. To apply these principles to the present situation, suppose that for the sake of argument I accept the official history propagated by Israel that the Zionist movement came in peace and that injustice was only perpetrated by Arabs against Jews. Suppose I accept the argument that in 1947 Palestinians rejected a generous UN partition plan that would have given them a state in 45 percent of their own country, and granted 55 percent to the Jewish minority, most of which had recently arrived from Europe—a plan that in hindsight they should have embraced. How does that help me deal with the fact that today approximately five million Jews and five million Palestinians live in that same country, the vast majority of whom were born after 1948? Should the supposed sins of the Palestinian fathers be visited on their children for generations to come? And if I take the view that Israel's Zionist founders intended only harm to the native population in whose country they came to establish a Jewish state, what then shall I do with their five million Jewish descendants? The fact is that today there are two communities who have a right to life, freedom, and absolute equality no matter what happened in the past or continues to happen in the present. If we start from this premise, reconciliation becomes conceivable, even possible.

It is a simple idea, but one that is painfully hard to implement, as the experience in Northern Ireland certainly demonstrates, because it means that some people with power will lose it and some without power will gain it. But it is also the fundamental principle behind the postapartheid dispensation in South Africa. After decades of the cruelty of apartheid and centuries of colonial exploitation, the people of that country, black and white, chose truth *and* reconciliation as the way forward. But the choice was not inevitable. The white government could have decided to use its overwhelming military resources to preserve its power for perhaps five, ten, or twenty more years. Black South Africans could have supported leaders who favored revenge instead of reconciliation. All of this might have led to millions of deaths and reduced the country to an ungovernable failed state of warring enclaves. At some point, some critical number of white South Africans, under intense internal and external pressure, realized that giving up power was the best way to secure their future, and that the possibility of an inclusive democracy offered the best guarantee of legitimacy, recognition, and inclusion as an integral part of South African society. It was crucial that the African National Congress, led by Nelson Mandela, was able to resist the Apartheid regime while at the same time appealing to the humanity of white South Africans, and convincing them that they had a place in the future.

My father spent nearly four decades as a diplomat working for peace. He believed in a two-state solution, one state for Israelis and one for Palestinians, based on UN resolutions. When he was Jordanian ambassador in Brussels, I often listened from behind the door as he briefed and argued with other ambassadors, politicians, and members of parliament, and I too became convinced that such a solution—while it did not mean justice for Palestinians—would nevertheless be a path to peace. Palestinians would not become Zionists, but they would accept the reality of the Jewish state and endeavor to live with it.

When the PLO formally recognized Israel within its internationally acknowledged borders and agreed to a two-state solution in 1993, like most Palestinians, I swallowed hard and accepted it. We believed that this unprecedented historic compromise, though bitter, was necessary. Those who rejected the creation of a state limited to the West Bank and Gaza Strip—a mere 22 percent of the country in which Palestinians were an overwhelming majority just forty-five years earlier—were relegated to the margins of the Palestinian movement.

Israel gave the world the impression it would agree to a Palestinian state and that it was only a matter of working out the technical formalities. But more than a decade later, Israel has still never fully recognized the Palestinian right to statehood, never committed to fully withdraw from the occupied territories, much less agreed to the creation of a truly independent and sovereign Palestine. On the contrary, in practice it has done everything to make the emergence of such a state impossible, by doubling the number of settlers in the occupied territories. Hundreds of thousands of Israeli Jews would need to be shifted from their current homes to reach an outcome that a minimum of Palestinians could agree to. Instead, Israel moved toward "unilateral disengagement"—essentially the nonnegotiated imposition of final borders—key elements of which, the isolation of Gaza and the construction of the separation wall in the West Bank, are experienced by Palestinians as apartheid.

Additionally, intense international focus on creating a Palestinian state in the occupied territories has obscured the existence of two important groups of Palestinians without whom there cannot be an end to the conflict. One is the citizens of Israel of Palestinian origin, who currently form 20 percent of the Israeli population, about 1.35 million Palestinians. The other group is the Palestinian refugees and exiles, who number more than 4 million. The creation of a Palestinian state even in all of the West Bank and Gaza Strip cannot resolve Israel's conflict with these two groups, who together constitute more than half of all Palestinians. The wrongs done to the Palestinian refugees and exiles cannot be redressed only through the creation of a Palestinian state. They are unlikely to forget about their homes and agree to resettle elsewhere with a new identity. While that would make life convenient for some, ending the conflict means dealing with the refugees as partners with a stake in a fair and sustainable resolution.

Given the current state of affairs, we are further away from achieving a two-state solution than ever. An increasing number of Palestinians, including some representatives of the Palestinian Authority, have thus started to talk once again about binationalism—the creation of a single democratic state for Israelis and Palestinians—as the only viable solution. While polls show that a majority of Palestinians support a two-state solution, their view shifts when they are given a choice only between the cantonization now being imposed and a single state shared with Israeli Jews. To Israelis, though, the idea is simply horrifying, a plot to destroy Israel: Most believe that only a monopoly on power in a democratic Jewish state with a Jewish majority can guarantee their safety.

Israel's "right" to be a Jewish state with a Jewish majority might be justifiable in the abstract, but cannot be implemented in practice without abandoning the most elementary democratic and human rights principles. If Israel truly had been established in a "land without a people," as traditional Zionist historiography holds, then its organization would be no one else's business, the concern only of the people who lived there.

But this was never the case. When a large non-Jewish population is not only present but indigenous, then Israel's right to a Jewish majority can be enforced only at the expense of the rights and basic existence of that population. In recent years, Israel has tried to delay the explosion of what it considers to be a "demographic time bomb"—a burgeoning Palestinian population combined with a decline in Jewish immigration—with policies that include encouraging immigration and discriminatory marriage and citizenship laws. Some parties have openly espoused "solutions" ranging from limiting the number of children that non-Jews are permitted to have to outright expulsion of the Palestinian population.[7] Both of these positions have gained in popularity, even though imposing reproductive limits on certain populations for political or ideological reasons and expelling undesired ethnic groups fall far outside the accepted norms of human morality and are universally condemned as crimes against humanity. The majority have responded to the demographic "time bomb" by endorsing unilateral separation, with its apartheid walls and regulations.

Israelis have been told for decades by their leaders that only an exclusive, Jewish-controlled enclave can guarantee their survival, and anything that threatens its existence in its present form threatens their very lives. But by maintaining this enclave at the expense of Palestinians, Israel has created many enemies. Palestinians too have committed acts that have only deepened Israeli hostility. At the same time, Palestinian nationalism, like the Zionism to which it is a response, is too narrow to accommodate the present reality of two deeply intertwined populations living on a small piece of land.

I believe that the majority of Israelis, even if they are alarmed by the logic of the "demographic threat" and persuaded by odious racist solutions like the marriage law or the disengagement plan, do aspire to progressive values, but these are not expressed in the state's actions. One can read the opinion polls showing growing Israeli support for expelling the Palestinians as a sign of implacable hatred, or one can interpret them as expressions of fear and desperation at the lack of any alternative to the failure thus far of the two-state solution.

In such a hopeless situation, clinging to the prospect of peace through a two-state solution becomes a valuable placebo against a painful reality, even if no serious effort is made to implement it. My father often tells the story of the caliph 'Umar ibn al-Khattab, who came across an impoverished woman with no food to feed her children, so she placed rocks in a pot of boiling water and stirred them constantly over the fire. Each time her children asked when the soup will be ready, she soothed them saying, "Soon, soon." The idea is that it is more bearable to live with the hope that one will eat than with the certainty that one will starve to death. The proliferation of peace plans and promises for a Palestinian state serve the same purpose, at best. At worst, they form a stage on which opportunists may strut around as peacemakers, knowing that their efforts will come to naught because they are unwilling to pay the political price of success. Anyone peering into the pot must see that if we keep stirring these rocks, we will die. We have to get up and look for something else. As the prospect of two states that will bring normality becomes increasingly faint, we are left only with hopelessness, hatred, extremist policies, and the prospect of endless, escalating violence as Israel tries to defend an unworkable dream against relentless reality.

Despite everything I know about the present state of affairs, I believe Israelis and Palestinians can live together in one country that they consider to be equally and simultaneously a Jewish state and a Palestinian state. This country will belong to all the people who live in it. It will provide a place for each of its communities to fulfill its national, cultural, and spiritual aspirations and needs. This country will take the best ideas and practices from successful multiethnic democracies like Belgium, India, Switzerland, Canada, and South Africa.

The time has come for an entirely different approach that starts from the premise that Israelis and Palestinians have equal rights. A perspective of equal rights leads inevitably to the conclusion that preserving a Jewish majority cannot be the goal of the peace process. Rather, the goal must be based on terms similar to those in the Good Friday Agreement. In practice, this means abandoning the quest for discrete ethnic-national states and looking for a model that allows both communities self-determination within a democracy.

My mother, God bless her, is still young and healthy and beautiful, but a day will come when there are no Palestinians left with a memory of peaceful coexistence between Jews and Arabs in Palestine before the creation of Israel. That memory is the key to a new future. Israelis and Palestinians need to withdraw from the dead end they have created, and they need help to do so, and they need to help each other. Many Israelis, and their American Jewish supporters, are driven by genuine, visceral fear but they need to listen to the few but powerful figures within and the many more without who understand that the current path leads to hell. Palestinians need to refocus efforts to build a broad campaign based on universal principles, one that protests repressive Israeli policies and mobilizes the worldwide support their cause does in fact enjoy. At the same time, they must reach out to Israelis with an inclusive vision of future reconciliation based on real equality.

The question here, then, is whether we can conceive of an alternative that leads us out of our current impasse, one that addresses the fears and needs of Israeli Jews, preserves their identity, and allows their community to flourish, while restoring to the Palestinians the rights they have been denied for so long. I believe there is a way forward that offers a real, tangible path to a future, to the creation of a normal country for Palestinians and Israelis. As difficult as it is to imagine these two peoples uniting to form a democratic state that includes and protects both, this is exactly what we need to do.

As I finished writing this book, Israel was engaged in a new war in Lebanon. Hundreds of thousands of Lebanese civilians were forced from their homes, and hundreds of children were among the civilians killed in the massive Israeli bombardment of Lebanese cities. Under barrages of retaliatory missiles fired from Lebanon, Israelis spoke of a sense of vulnerability they had not experienced in decades. This war, however it ends, will only harden the feelings that have brought us to this point: Israel as a "Jewish state" maintained at the expense of Palestinians and other Arabs enjoys less acceptance and faces stiffer resistance among peoples of the region than ever, while Israeli Jews increasingly believe that only overwhelming military can guarantee their survival. When the smoke clears, we will again see clearly that this war, like those before it, is a direct consequence of the unresolved conflict between Israelis and Palestinians, one to which there can be no solution based on force.

I believe that despite heightened emotions and greater bitterness on all sides, the discussion this book seeks to widen is more urgent than ever and its conclusion only more valid: one state for both peoples. For the many who doubt this is possible, I ask you only to walk with me a little, to give it your consideration.

CHAPTER ONE

An Impossible Partition

U K foreign secretary Jack Straw stood at the dispatch box
in a packed House of Commons. After parrying members' questions on the intricacies of European Union (EU)
budgetary reform and sugar subsidies, he became more ebul-
lient when debate turned to the Middle East peace process. He
commended Prime Minister Ariel Sharon for his "courage" in
pulling Israeli settlers out of Gaza and declared, "I am more
hopeful about the prospects for a lasting peace between Israel and
the Palestinians than I have been at any time in the past four and
a half years." Straw boomed, "I believe that gradually both sides
have recognized that the only future for Palestinians and Israelis
lies in peace and in two states."[1] Straw could have learned something from those who had stood at the dispatch box before him. It
was the British government after all, one still flush with colonial
territories, that had in the 1930s first given its official imprimatur
to partition as *the* solution to the conflict between Jews and Arabs
in Palestine. Partition failed then, as it is failing again today, as it
has failed every time it has been seriously proposed, always for

the same reason: There is no workable partition that is acceptable to a majority of Israelis and Palestinians.

Partition of Palestine into one homeland for Jews and another for Arabs was first endorsed as a government plan in 1937. That year, the Palestine Royal Commission, headed by Lord Peel, formed after disturbances in Palestine and the outbreak of the Arab revolt, proposed to divide the country into two states, with the British retaining control of Jerusalem and a corridor leading to the port of Jaffa. The proposed Jewish state would include all of the Galilee in the north and the coastal plain down to the south of Tel Aviv. The Arab state would comprise all the rest of the country. Even with this plan, expectations of settling on a fair border between the two entities were low. "No frontier can be drawn," the report warned, "which separates all Arabs and Arab-owned land from all Jews and Jewish-owned land." The problem was the Arabs, or more specifically, the quantity of them: There were simply too many. While the area allocated for the Arab state would have contained only 1,250 Jews, the Jewish state would have contained more than a quarter of a million Arabs. "It is the far greater number of Arabs who constitute the major problem," the report concluded. Because it was impossible to construct a viable Jewish state given these facts, the Peel Commission recommended solving the demographic "problem" through the removal, "voluntary or otherwise," of all Arabs from the proposed Jewish state not just to other parts of Palestine, but even across the frontier to Transjordan (modern-day Jordan), a solution that today would properly be called ethnic cleansing.[2]

A year after its release, the Woodhead Commission scuttled the Peel plan because it found that, at a minimum, the proposed

Jewish state would have an Arab population of 49 percent. The commissioners could not agree on any other partition scheme, and one member concluded that no form of partition was practicable.[3] In 1939, the British government issued a new White Paper on Palestine that also reversed the Peel Commission's key findings. Instead of partition, it endorsed a unitary state in which Arabs and Jews would have equal rights.

The next serious proposal for partition, and the most detailed, came almost a decade later. Toward the end of British rule in Palestine, granted by a League of Nations mandate, the British were losing control of the population and so handed the problem to the newly formed United Nations. In 1947, the United Nations Special Committee on Palestine (UNSCOP), composed of representatives of eleven states, recommended the partition of the country into independent Jewish and Arab states. A majority of the countries in UNSCOP (Canada, Czechoslovakia, Guatemala, Netherlands, Peru, Sweden, and Uruguay) voted for partition, while the minority (India, Iran, and Yugoslavia) proposed a single, federal binational state. Australia abstained. On November 29, 1947, the UN General Assembly accepted the UNSCOP majority recommendation, Resolution 181, by a vote of 33–13 with 10 abstentions. Mainstream Zionist leaders endorsed the plan, but most did so "with a heavy heart" out of opposition to the idea of a Palestinian state and a desire for control over a greater area of territory.[4] David Ben-Gurion, in his testimony to UNSCOP, had argued against partition because he believed that the entire country should be given to the Jews. He urged postponement of any decision until the Jews, by encouraging immigration, could become the majority and thus take control of all the country.[5] Nevertheless once the plan was passed by the General Assembly, Zionist leaders hailed it as a major diplomatic achievement, and there was widespread celebration in the Jewish community in Palestine and among Zionist supporters around the world.

While international opinion was coalescing around UN plans for partition, the voices of those who would be most affected—Palestinians—had little bearing on the deliberations. Arab leaders in Palestine and Arab states rejected the UN plan. They had proposed to UNSCOP that Palestine be given its independence as a unitary state, that there be a constituent assembly made of Arabs and Jews, that Jews participate fully in its government under proportional representation, and that Jewish immigration be curbed to prevent a Jewish takeover and the loss of the "Arab character" of Palestine.[6] Even today, Palestinian speakers, including myself, are often challenged with the claim that had the Palestinians only accepted the UN plan they would by now have enjoyed their freedom and independence for nearly sixty years. But such twenty-twenty hindsight does little to illuminate the reality Palestinians faced. My father, who was twelve years old at the time, remembers that even in his small, rural village there was lively concern over the UNSCOP partition plan. Palestinians were universally against partition for two reasons. He explains: "First, they thought, you don't partition what's yours. They didn't see their rights to Palestine as disputable, so they did not see partition as a reasonable compromise. And also we knew—even as little children—and I remember talking about it, that if the Jews accepted partition it would only be as a foothold for taking the rest of Palestine later." Palestinians simply didn't see why towns and villages a short distance away and to which they had deep ties should suddenly, by the decree of a distant body, be placed out of their reach behind international borders. It was simply inconceivable. Palestinians were being given hardly anything in the partition; they were losing more than half their country.

Even if people could have been brought to see partition as reasonable in theory, the terms proposed by UNSCOP added insult to injury. In 1947, there were 1,293,000 Arab Palestinians—Muslims and Christians—and 608,000 Jews in the country. Although Jews were one-third of the population, most had arrived only recently after fleeing the horrors of World War II, and Zionist efforts to buy up the country had met with some resistance. The result was Jews owned about 6 percent of the land.[7] Nevertheless, the partition resolution proposed to give Jews 55 percent of the country. The Palestinians, who were two-thirds of the population and owned the vast majority of the land, which they had been working for generations, were to make do with less than half of the country. Jerusalem would be declared an international zone. An example of the inequity in this is UNSCOP's decision that "the Jews will have the more economically developed part of the country embracing practically the whole of the citrus-producing area which includes a large number of Arab producers."[8]

As the Peel Commission had found a decade earlier, a truly workable partition was impossible: Both of the proposed states were each to be broken into three awkwardly separated sections, while the Jewish and Arab blocs would be untidily intertwined. The Jewish state proposed by UNSCOP would have contained 498,000 Jews, but also 407,000 Arabs (not including 90,000 nomadic Bedouins)—nearly half of the population— raising fears among Palestinians that the Arabs whose homes were inside the designated Jewish areas might be forcibly removed as the Peel Commission had recommended. The proposed Arab state would have contained 725,000 Palestinians and just 10,000 Jews, while there would be roughly 105,000 non-Jews and 100,000 Jews in the Jerusalem international zone.[9]

Reading the UN records and debates, it is clear that the UNSCOP plan was adopted with misgivings and with recognition of at least some of its shortcomings, but what animated its strongest proponents was sympathy with Zionist claims for undivided Jewish sovereignty over a substantial part, if not all, of Palestine and a desire to solve the problem of Jewish refugees that had been created by Germany's extermination of millions of European Jews. Even for those who saw the issues of Jewish refugees in Europe and the question of Palestine as distinct, the plan had the attraction of appearing to be final. The UNSCOP majority recognized that "partition has been strongly opposed by Arabs, but it is felt that opposition would be lessened by a solution which definitely fixes the extent of territory to be allotted to the Jews with its implicit limitation on immigration. The fact that the solution carries the sanction of the United Nations involves a finality which should allay Arab fears of further expansion of the Jewish State."[10] Just like the Peel Commission, the UNSCOP majority believed that partition, though far from perfect, offered the chance of eventual peace.

The UN partition plan was never implemented. Fighting between Jews and Arabs broke out the day after its approval.

Arab protestors attacked Jewish areas, and within weeks the Haganah, the Jewish military, began well-planned operations to conquer territory well beyond that which the partition resolution granted. The war of 1947–48 resulted in the partition of Palestine by force, rather than agreement, leaving 78 percent of the territory in Israeli hands, with the remaining 22 percent— East Jerusalem, the West Bank and Gaza Strip—under Jordanian and Egyptian rule respectively. Fewer than 180,000 Palestinians remained behind in the newly declared State of Israel, while between 700,000 and 900,000 were displaced to the West Bank and Gaza Strip or became refugees in surrounding countries.

There was little more talk of partition and a separate Palestinian state until after the war in 1967 when Israel militarily occupied East Jerusalem, the West Bank, Gaza Strip, Syria's Golan Heights, and Egypt's Sinai Peninsula. The UN Security Council adopted Resolution 242, which remains the basis of the current consensus for a solution. Resolution 242 emphasizes "the inadmissibility of the acquisition of territory by war and the need to work for a just and lasting peace in which every State in the area can live in security"—what has come to be known in shorthand as the "land for peace" formula. In exchange for Israeli withdrawal from the occupied territories, Arab states would recognize Israel, sign peace agreements, and establish normal relations. It was many years before either Israel or the Palestinian national movement was prepared to say it accepted this principle.

With the signing of the 1993 Oslo Accords, the Palestinian leadership recognized Israel explicitly and limited its demands to the creation of a Palestinian state only in the West Bank and

Gaza, an enormous compromise given that these lands constitute just a fifth of the whole country in which Palestinians had
been the overwhelming majority. The accords also affirmed the
general terms of limited Palestinian self-rule in Gaza and the
West Bank. But Israelis and Palestinians deferred all decisions
on so-called final status issues, including defining borders, the
fate of settlements, Jerusalem, and refugees. At the time, it was
impossible to narrow the vast gaps between the two sides. Various "confidence-building measures" were supposed to set the
stage for agreement later on. Unfortunately, confidence only
sank as developments on the ground made the unbridgeable
gaps of 1993 even wider.

Months after the 1967 war, Israel began moving settlers into the
West Bank and Gaza Strip in direct violation of the Fourth
Geneva Convention, which states that an "Occupying Power
shall not deport or transfer parts of its own civilian population
into the territory it occupies." This policy was for decades
implemented by both Labor- and Likud-led governments. It was
an explicit attempt by successive Israeli governments to change
the demographic and geographic realities in the occupied territories, and ultimately force the world to accept permanent Israeli
control over them as a fait accompli. The ambition was expanded
in 1977 when Ariel Sharon, newly appointed agriculture minister, set in motion a plan to settle two million Jews in the
occupied territories by the end of the twentieth century, including settlements in Syria's Golan Heights and in Egypt's Sinai

Peninsula (which was returned as part of Israel's peace treaty with Egypt).[11] Sharon and his associates planned what they called a "demographic transformation" that would result in a Jewish majority across the 1967 border. Mattiyahu Drobles, co-chairman of the Jewish Agency's Settlement Department, responsible for implementation of the plan, explained in May 1979: "[T]he state of Israel must for political and other reasons, develop the entire region of Judea and Samaria;[12] and if in five years' time, 100,000 Jews will not live in this region, I doubt that we will have a right to this region. If Jews will live in Judea and Samaria it will be ours; if they will not live there, it will not."[13]

Drobles asserted that the settlements should be strategically positioned in "the areas between and around the centers occupied by" Palestinians "to reduce to a minimum the danger of an additional Arab state being established in these territories. Being cut off by Jewish settlements, the minority population will find it difficult to form a territorial and political continuity."[14] His use of the word "minorities" to describe the Palestinians, even though they were and still are the overwhelming majority in the areas targeted by this program, was more a reference to intention rather than an acknowledgment of truth.

Although Israel had not met the goal of outnumbering Palestinians in the West Bank, the results of the settlement effort are impressive by any standard and have created—as planners intended—an irreversible reality. By constructing settlements, as well as an extensive road network connecting them to Israeli cities, Israel has fragmented contiguous Palestinian territory into dozens of isolated patches in which the vast majority of Palestinians are corralled. Their freedom of movement is restricted by walls, fences, and army checkpoints that turn the simplest excursion into an arduous expedition that may require detours of hours, if it is achievable at all.

In the two decades from 1972 to 1993, Israel increased the number of settlers in the West Bank, not including Jerusalem, from 800 to 111,600. In the following ten years—which roughly coincided with the Oslo peace process—the number increased at twice the rate, exceeding 234,000 by 2004.[15] In East Jerusalem, the settler population jumped from 124,400 in 1992 to almost 176,000 in 2002.[16] Overall, the settler population now exceeds 400,000. The settlements and their attendant infrastructure and Jewish-only connecting highways control 42 percent of the West Bank, according to Israel's human rights organization B'Tselem.[17]

The colonization program has affected every part of the West Bank and Gaza, but has been particularly focused on Jerusalem. After the 1967 war, Prime Minister Golda Meir instructed her officials to strictly limit the Arab percentage of the city's population to no more than 28.8 percent in order to bolster Israel's claim to sovereignty over the conquered city.[18] Israel expropriated massive tracts of Palestinian-owned land. According to Amir Cheshin and Avi Melamed, successive advisers to Israeli-imposed Jerusalem mayors Teddy Kollek and Ehud Olmert, the intention of the policy has been "rapidly to increase the Jewish population in East Jerusalem" and "to hinder the growth of the Arab population and to force Arab residents to make their homes elsewhere," often under the banal guise of "urban planning."[19] A standard Israeli method for try-ing to force the growing Palestinian population out of the city was by systematically denying it building permits. In some neighborhoods it was illegal for Palestinians to build a single home even though ample space existed for them to do so.[20] These policies of demographic gerrymandering and involuntary displacement continue to be strictly implemented. In mid-2005, for example, Israel announced that it would destroy eighty-eight homes in the Silwan area of East Jerusalem, making 1,000 Palestinians homeless. The rationale for the demolition of the homes Israel declared "unauthorized" was to create an "archaeological" park on the site Jews claim as the ancient city of King David. One of the elderly homeowners, Hashim Jalajil, contemplating the demolition of the house he was born in seventy-six years previously, protested, "How can they build a garden for a man who died thousands of years ago? What, is King David going to come here and drink coffee? I now have 50 people to look after, aged from 2 to 51 years old. Where are we going to go?"[21] After international criticism, the municipality put the demolitions on hold but did not cancel the plan. Palestinians in East Jerusalem, where Israeli authorities demolished two hundred other homes in 2004–5, making 600 Palestinians homeless,[22] feared this was simply a temporary reprieve that would be lifted once the furor died down.

As thousands of journalists descended on the Gaza Strip in August 2005 to broadcast the scenes of Jewish settlers being dragged away by unarmed Israeli soldiers, many commentators hoped that the much-vaunted "disengagement" demonstrated that the facts on the ground created by Israel since 1967 are indeed reversible. As traumatic as the pullout was for Israelis, they argued, it broke an important taboo. Many Israeli leftists who once demonized Ariel Sharon enthusiastically embraced neighborhoods it was illegal for Palestinians to build a single home even though ample space existed for them to do so.[20] These policies of demographic gerrymandering and involuntary displacement continue to be strictly implemented. In mid-2005, for example, Israel announced that it would destroy eighty-eight homes in the Silwan area of East Jerusalem, making 1,000 Palestinians homeless. The rationale for the demolition of the homes Israel declared "unauthorized" was to create an "archaeological" park on the site Jews claim as the ancient city of King David. One of the elderly homeowners, Hashim Jalajil, contemplating the demolition of the house he was born in seventy-six years previously, protested, "How can they build a garden for a man who died thousands of years ago? What, is King David going to come here and drink coffee? I now have 50 people to look after, aged from 2 to 51 years old. Where are we going to go?"[21] After international criticism, the municipality put the demolitions on hold but did not cancel the plan. Palestinians in East Jerusalem, where Israeli authorities demolished two hundred other homes in 2004–5, making 600 Palestinians homeless,[22] feared this was simply a temporary reprieve that would be lifted once the furor died down.

As thousands of journalists descended on the Gaza Strip in August 2005 to broadcast the scenes of Jewish settlers being dragged away by unarmed Israeli soldiers, many commentators hoped that the much-vaunted "disengagement" demonstrated that the facts on the ground created by Israel since 1967 are indeed reversible. As traumatic as the pullout was for Israelis, they argued, it broke an important taboo. Many Israeli leftists who once demonized Ariel Sharon enthusiastically embraced him, believing that he was the Israeli De Gaulle who would begin to reverse the colonization he had devoted his political life to masterminding.

Ghassan Khatib, then Palestinian Authority minister of labor, lamented in the run-up to the Gaza settler pullout that "while talking about vacating settlements with less than 2,000 housing units in Gaza, Israel has been busy constructing, this year alone, something like 6,400 housing units in illegal settlements in the West Bank, mostly centered on Jerusalem."[23] Many Palestinians, like Khatib, suspected that the Gaza plan was just a smokescreen for intensified colonization in the West Bank. Prior to the supposed disengagement, it was fair to counter such skepticism by arguing that politically speaking, it was as much as any Israeli leader could do to take eight thousand settlers out of Gaza. To place additional pressure on Israel before the Gaza withdrawal would have been futile and possibly counterproductive. The time to test Israel's intentions and those of the international community was after completion of the settler pullout.

Within weeks, Israeli authorities announced plans for thousands of new settler homes all across the West Bank, including 3,500 as part of E-1, a program to expand Ma'ale Adumim, already the largest settlement. When completed, E-1 will permanently break the north-south contiguity of the West Bank. Michael Tarazi, then legal adviser to the Palestinian Authority's minister for Jerusalem affairs, protested that the land slated for E-1 constituted "the last undeveloped area that provides access for Palestinians in east Jerusalem to the rest of the occupied territories," while Dror Etkes, a settlement expert with the group Peace Now, said that building in E-1 "is tantamount to greater Palestinian autonomy, dozens of Israeli military check-points and hundreds of unmanned roadblocks have sprouted between Palestinian towns and cities, choking that autonomy. The number of physical obstacles to Palestinian movement placed by the Israeli army in the West Bank stood at 376 in August 2005 and rose to 471 in January 2006—a 25 percent increase in the six months after the Gaza disengagement.[26] Many of the manned checkpoints have evolved into vast, permanent structures. The construction of a new multimillion-dollar Israeli border police terminal at Qalandia in the West Bank, between Ramallah and East Jerusalem, prompted one Palestinian to lament that soon "the seemingly innocuous-sounding words 'checkpoint' and 'roadblock' will be transformed into a respectable, legitimate-looking border crossing, a fact on the ground as solid as the long concrete wall it faces."[27]

Israel's separation wall snakes for hundreds of kilometers through the West Bank, slicing streets down the middle, dividing villages, cutting families off from each other, students from their schools, doctors and patients from hospitals, and farmers from their crops. John Dugard, a South African lawyer and former member of that country's postapartheid Truth and Reconciliation Commission, wrote in his capacity as the United Nations Special Rapporteur on human rights in the occupied territories that the impact of the wall and "the restrictions on freedom of movement imposed by the Israeli authorities on Palestinians resemble the notorious 'pass laws' of apartheid South Africa and in some respects went far beyond them since the apartheid regime never had roads reserved for whites." He points out that "[m]any roads in the West Bank are set aside for the exclusive use of Jewish settlers."[28] One farmer, Sharif Omar of Jayyous in the West Bank, explained the impact of the wall on his family in Simone Bitton's film *Wall* (2005):

I have four daughters and three sons. All of them have university degrees, praise be to God, thanks to the income from my land. Today, I fear the Israelis will take my land away. I have 2,700 [fruit and olive] trees on the other side of the wall.

Like millions of other Palestinians in the West Bank, Omar is unable to cross the wall except through gates that are few and far between, and which are rarely and irregularly opened by the army. Omar echoed the view of many Palestinians when he observed:

The Israeli army claims that the wall will guarantee the security of both peoples. I cannot see how they plan to bring security to both peoples when they are not building on the Green Line [1967 border], which we see as a polit-ical boundary. They push the wall six kilometers into Jayyous. How can this provide security? They dig 28 meters from our homes and they say the wall is supposed "to prevent the touch between the two peoples." We were six kilometers away and now we are 28 meters away! It's a big lie. The truth is they want to expropriate our land. It is an indirect way to try to get us to abandon our villages. How? Because if they take our land and leave us with nothing to make a living, to feed our children and grandchildren, we will have to leave to look for work elsewhere. In practice, it is an expulsion operation in disguise, so that the world can continue to praise Israel or be silent and treat us like terrorists.

Peace Now confirmed Omar's fears when it reported that "the main building effort in the Jewish settlements in the West Bank is now focused on the area between the Green Line and the separation fence, and it is aimed at turning the fence into Israel's permanent border."[29] The UN and human rights organizations have estimated that up to 800,000 Palestinians will be directly and adversely affected by the wall. The International Court of Justice (ICJ) ruled the wall illegal in July 2004 chiefly because it recognized that "the construction of the wall and its associated regime create a *fait accompli* on the ground that could well become permanent, in which case, . . . [it] would be tantamount to *de facto* annexation" of vast areas of Palestinian land.[30] The accumulated result of Israel's settlement policies, says Israeli anthropologist Jeff Halper, is the "reconfiguration of the country from two parallel north-south units—Israel and the West Bank, the basis of the two-state idea—into one country, integrated east-west," that simply cannot be partitioned.[31]

The implications of recognizing that Israel has or is about to render a two-state solution practically impossible are enormous, which is perhaps why diplomats continue to exude escapist optimism about the prospects for peace. Nonetheless, public spin aside, the ramifications of Israel's unchecked expansionism are being noticed. A leaked 2004 secret report by the UK's Department for International Development and the Foreign Office stated, "Without action soon, there is a real danger that facts on the ground may make a viable two-state solution almost impossible."[32] Given this realization, could any action from the international community or from within Palestine save the possibility of partition?

Many Palestinian rights activists hailed the 2004 decision by the ICJ ruling the Israeli wall illegal and ordering its removal as a major victory. Indeed, the decision, which came in response to a Palestinian petition, confirmed the international consensus in support of Palestinian self-determination and Israel's withdrawal from the occupied territories, essentially a consensus on a two-state resolution of the conflict. But this consensus has now been in existence for decades, and its reaffirmation in the world court seems unlikely to indicate any serious action by governments to implement it.

Almost twenty-five years before the ICJ issued its verdict, the UN Security Council, in Resolution 465 (1980), determined "that all measures taken by Israel to change the physical character, demographic composition, institutional structure, or status of the Palestinian and other Arab territories occupied since 1967, including Jerusalem, or any part thereof, have no legal validity and that Israel's policy and practices of settling parts of its population and new immigrants in those territories constitute a flagrant violation of the Fourth Geneva Convention relative to the Protection of Civilian Persons in Time of War and also constitute a serious obstruction to achieving a comprehensive, just and lasting peace in the Middle East." The resolution called "upon the Government and people of Israel to rescind those measures, to dismantle the existing settlements and in particular to cease, on an urgent basis, the establishment, construction and planning of settlements," and called upon all UN Member States "not to provide Israel with any assistance to be used specifically in connection with settlements in the occupied territories." This resolution was not unique. In Resolution 476 of 1980, the Security Council reaffirmed "the overriding necessity to end the prolonged occupation of Arab territories occupied by Israel since 1967, including Jerusalem," and stated its "determination in the event of non-compliance by Israel with this resolution, to examine practical ways and means in accordance with relevant provisions of the Charter of the United Nations to secure the full implementation of this resolution." What could be clearer than that? And yet here we are four decades into the occupation, and never has the United Nations taken a single "practical" measure to halt or reverse any of Israel's ongoing violations.

Today there is even less willingness by governments to confront Israel and hold it accountable. The reason that the Palestinians had to go to the ICJ in the first place—to seek an advisory opinion restating what had already been said—is that the Security Council will neither pass new resolutions nor see to it that old yet valid resolutions are implemented. Not only do the powerful states on the Security Council block action to enforce Palestinian rights and punish Israeli violations, but the United States and virtually all the EU countries opposed the Palestinian decision to take their case to the ICJ.

Some commentators compared the ICJ's ruling on the West Bank wall to its 1971 decision that South Africa's occupation of Namibia was illegal. That decision was a prelude to international sanctions against the Pretoria government. Sanctions did not materialize in response to the court ruling itself, but as a result of broad and active diplomatic and political campaigns to isolate the apartheid regime. The question for Palestinians is not whether they have a court decision or a Security Council resolution upholding their claims—they have always had that—but whether they have the political clout to turn these decisions into actions. Over time, international law has been increasingly marginalized as a basis for resolving the conflict. Israel has sought to sideline it. The United Nations has now been pushed aside in favor of the Quartet, an ad hoc body made up of U.S., Russian, and EU representatives, and the secretary-general of the UN. Though this group provides a semblance of international sponsorship for Palestinian-Israeli peacemaking, in practice it has been dominated by the United States and has placed no check on Israeli settlement construction.

The resort to the ICJ did confirm the strength of the Palestinians' legal case, but it also proved just how little political support they have to get their rights implemented through international bodies. International law is simply powerless unless the political will exists to enforce it by compelling an offending country to comply.

*   *   *

Aaron Miller, a twenty-five-year veteran of the State Department and a key official during the failed Camp David summit in July 2000, reflected in 2005 that "[f]or far too long, many American officials involved in Arab-Israeli peacemaking, myself included, have acted as Israel's attorney, catering and coordinating with the Israelis at the expense of successful peace negotiations."[33] Miller's mea culpa was not the first such declaration, and like those of other officials who have said similar things, he waited until he was retired to speak out—until it made no difference.

For decades, Palestinian leaders pinned their strategy for a Palestinian state on the hope that the United States would eventually apply the necessary pressure on Israel to end the occupation and remove the settlements: Since the United States stands in the way of international action to force Israel to withdraw from the occupied territories, then Palestinians ought to try to influence the United States. How realistic is this strategy?

The first and only time the United States decisively challenged Israel was after Israel, in concert with Great Britain and France, invaded Egypt in 1956. The Eisenhower administration forcefully insisted that the Israeli occupation of Sinai was illegal and under U.S. pressure Israel pulled out unconditionally. If Eisenhower's successors had stuck to his policies, the United States might have maintained and increased the widespread popularity it enjoyed in the Arab world in the years after World War II as a country that was seen to stand for fairness, democracy, and a clean break from the colonial policies of European powers that had bedeviled the region for so long.

From Eisenhower's tough stance in 1956, the erosion of U.S. support for international law as the basis for peace in the Middle East was gradual but relentless. U.S. economic, military, and diplomatic aid to Israel increased dramatically after 1967 as policymakers saw Israel as an ally in the Cold War. Nevertheless, from the beginning of the 1967 occupation through the Carter administration, the United States, like virtually every other government in the world, viewed the Israeli settlements as illegal.[34] During the Reagan and George H. W. Bush administrations, the U.S. position was softened so that the settlements were described only as "obstacles to peace." After the signing of the Oslo Accords, President Bill Clinton and his officials diluted the position even further, typically referring to the settlements as merely "unhelpful." Under President George W. Bush, the United States has openly endorsed the settlements.

President Bush made his first major foray into the conflict with a Rose Garden speech on June 24, 2002. His much anticipated intervention weighed in at 1,867 words. By my count, more than 1,000 words were devoted to criticizing and making demands of the Palestinians, while just 137 words dealt with what Israel should do. There was no criticism of Israeli actions whatsoever. The speech was so unbalanced that *Jerusalem Report* editor David Horowitz told National Public Radio that the Sharon government "might almost feel that they could have drafted it themselves."[35] Bush entirely accepted the Israeli view that "terror" alone was the source of the conflict. In Bush's conception, it was up to the Palestinians to "reform" themselves before any demands, no matter how mild, could be made of Israel.

Given this ominous start, Palestinians were apprehensive when Bush unveiled his Road Map peace plan in April 2003. But the Road Map did not confirm their worst fears. Holding out the prospect of "a final and comprehensive settlement of the Israel-Palestinian conflict by 2005," the plan reaffirmed the need to "end the occupation that began in 1967, based on the foundations of the Madrid Conference, the principle of land for peace," and in accordance with UN resolutions. Phase one of the Quartet-endorsed Road Map seemed eminently reasonable and if it did not spell out solutions to all contentious issues, it was still a good place to start. At the outset, the plan demanded from the Palestinian leadership an "unequivocal statement reiterating Israel's right to exist in peace and security and calling for an immediate and unconditional ceasefire to end armed activity and all acts of violence against Israelis anywhere." Israel was required to issue an "unequivocal statement affirming its commitments to the two-state vision of an independent, viable, sovereign Palestinian state living in peace and security alongside Israel," and to observe "an immediate end to violence against Palestinians everywhere." Simultaneously, Israel was to freeze all settlement construction including what it claimed was "natural growth" within the boundaries of already existing settlements. Yet after launching the Road Map to great international fanfare and optimism, Bush quickly gutted it of its useful content by acceding to pressure from Israel and its political allies that all Israeli actions should be conditioned on prior Palestinian action. Bush made increasingly strident demands of the Palestinians while Israel's obligations were ignored.

A year later, President Bush dropped a bombshell, assuring

Israel that the United States would back its demand that any final peace settlement would leave the major settlement blocs in Israeli hands forever. "In light of new realities on the ground, including already existing major Israeli population centers," Bush wrote to Prime Minister Ariel Sharon, "it is unrealistic to expect that the outcome of final status negotiations will be a full and complete return to the armistice lines" that defined Israel's borders until the 1967 war.[36]

Palestinian leaders and observers around the world were deeply dismayed, and reacted as if Bush's assurance had been a great departure from recent U.S. policy. Yes, Bush was abandoning the core of the Road Map, but it had been the Road Map, with its uncharacteristic evenhandedness, that had been the short-lived departure. Bush's letter to Sharon did little that Bush's predecessor had not already done. In a speech to the Israel Policy Forum on January 7, 2001 in the final weeks of his term, and in writing to Israeli and Palestinian leaders shortly before he left office, President Clinton had explicitly endorsed "the incorporation into Israel of settlement blocks."[37] Bush was simply renewing the signal to Israel that it could predetermine the outcome of any negotiation by creating new realities on the ground.

Reflecting the solid, bipartisan consensus behind the Bush-Clinton green light to the settlements, the U.S. House of Representatives voted 407–9 in June 2004 to endorse Bush's letter of assurances. During the 2004 presidential election campaign that summer, Bush and his Democratic challenger, Senator John Kerry, clashed on many issues, but not on Palestine-Israel. This is good politics in America but disastrous policy. Today

Israel remains a taboo subject and any politician who wishes to see his or her career flourish knows better than to speak out against its policies. Hillary Clinton learned that lesson the hard way. Castigated as first lady for expressing sentiments in favor of a Palestinian state, she has become one of the leading pro-Israel hawks as a U.S. senator from New York.

The core of support for America's pro-Israel policies may be found in communities that are well-organized and highly influential through national lobbying groups such as the American Israel Public Affairs Committee (AIPAC), the Anti-Defamation League (ADL), and countless local counterparts that channel campaign donations to friendly candidates and punish perceived opponents. The prevailing views of American Jews are reflected in U.S. policy. While support for a Palestinian state has consistently grown and was at 56 percent in 2005, according to the American Jewish Committee's *Annual Survey of American Jewish Opinion,* only 15 percent of American Jews believes Israel should withdraw from all the settlements, and fewer than half believes Israel should withdraw from any settlements. Three-fifths of American Jews oppose any compromise over Jerusalem. Thus there does not appear to be a large constituency among American Jews to put real pressure on Israel, especially since leaders of communal organizations and the most activist Jews tend to be more hard-line. While American Jews have traditionally supported the Democratic Party, pro-Israel sentiment has recently taken a much firmer hold in the Republican Party as Christian fundamentalists have become its active support base. Religious leaders such as Pat Robertson, who warned President Bush that any pressure on Israel to relinquish occupied territories would interfere with "God's plan," have become increasingly vocal.[38]

Some Palestinian Americans believe that their lack of influence on U.S. policymaking could be redressed by intensified efforts to emulate pro-Israel lobby groups who have wielded such great influence on U.S. politicians, and they decry what they see as a lack of participation by their community. However, the trajectory of Barack Obama of Illinois is instructive in this regard. In the 2004 elections, Illinois swept Obama, a rising star in the Democratic Party, into the United States Senate with a stunning 70 percent of the vote—a rare Democratic gain. He participated in many events in the Chicago-area Arab community, including a 1998 fund-raiser for an Arab American community organization where Edward Said was the keynote speaker.

Obama's criticism of U.S. policy in the Middle East at private fund-raisers suggested the emergence of someone who would finally speak for evenhanded U.S. policies toward Israelis and Palestinians. Because of these positions, and no less because of his progressive stances on economic and social justice in the United States, Obama was the first U.S. politician who inspired me to pull out my checkbook.

But after Obama's nationally televised address at the 2004 Democratic National Convention in Boston, everything seemed to change. Obama became a media darling and the new hope of the floundering Democratic Party. In the campaign's final weeks, he started to sound like a mainstream hawk, proclaiming his support for tough sanctions and military strikes against Iran if it refused U.S. demands to give up its nuclear energy program.

Dropping the criticism of Israel, Obama declared that the onus for peace in the Middle East "is on the Palestinian leadership, which . . . must cease violence against Israelis and work to end the incitement against Israel in the Arab world."[39] His thoughtful analysis had gone out the window and been replaced by talking points that could have been written by any of the major pro-Israel lobby groups.

As Obama eased into his role as senator, and was increasingly tipped as a possible running mate for Hillary Clinton in 2008, his public statements were at times even more hard-line than those made by the Bush administration. During a January 2006 visit to Israel, for example, he opposed allowing Palestinians in occupied East Jerusalem to vote in Palestinian Authority legislative elections, even after the Bush administration urged Israel to allow the election to proceed.[40] So, if a man like Obama will not speak frankly on Israel for fear that it might cost him political capital, what hope is there for any change in U.S. policy coming from within? Obama's politically expedient about-face and the lack of any real political debate over U.S. support for Israel suggests that a shift in policy, if not impossible to achieve through direct participation in electoral politics, would take decades—and that will simply be too late.

Other sources of diplomatic pressure on Israel seem to offer equally slim hopes. For many years, Palestinians looked to the European Union or the United Nations, also members of the Quartet, to provide an independent counterbalance to U.S. bias toward Israel. Unfortunately, both bodies have abandoned any attempt to play such a role. One crucial test came in May 2004, when Israel embarked on the wide-scale destruction of homes in the Rafah refugee camp in the Gaza Strip. United Nations relief officials reported that in just over three weeks, Israeli army bulldozers had leveled 277 houses, making 3,451 Palestinians homeless.[41] Many human rights groups condemned the demolitions as war crimes, including B'Tselem, which declared that "such massive destructions of civilian property are illegal under international humanitarian law," and that the deaths of Israeli occupation soldiers "cannot justify the severe harm to civilians, who were not involved in the hostilities."[42]

As the demolitions went on and dozens of Palestinian civilians in Rafah were killed by Israeli forces, the Quartet's inaction became increasingly perplexing and embarrassing. UN secretary-general Kofi Annan was asked why the Quartet did nothing to stop the Israeli attacks. He acknowledged, "You would want to see immediate action by the Quartet . . . to stop the demolition of the houses, and that is going to take the kind of action and will and resources and confrontation that quite frankly, today, I don't see anyone in the international community willing to take."[43] After the demolitions were over, several governments donated millions of dollars to rebuild many of the destroyed homes. Another stark example came in July–August 2006 when key actors refused to call for a ceasefire in the Israeli air assault that killed hundreds of Lebanese civilians and destroyed their country's infrastructure. This silence in the face of Israeli crimes, and willingness to clean up the mess, follows a pattern and has prompted many Palestinians to feel that international aid uncoupled from pressure on the Israelis simply prolongs, not alleviates, their misery. Palestinian Authority information consultant and author Ghada Karmi has challenged donors "to consider that Israel's occupation of Palestine is set to continue so long as they remain prepared to underwrite it."[44] Palestinians have unsuccessfully called on the EU, Israel's largest trading partner, to take effective action against abuses that European officials have long recognized and condemned. Under the terms of its Association Agreement with the EU, Israel benefits from preferential access to European markets. The trade accord states that its application "shall be based on respect for human rights and democratic principles which . . . constitute an essential element of this agreement." Yet the EU has never enforced this part of the agreement.

Ironically, when the EU and other Quartet members did finally get around to imposing economic sanctions it was against not Israel but the Palestinians, after Hamas's victory in general elections in January 2006. Hamas leaders reflected widespread Palestinian sentiment when they pointed out that the Quartet operated according to a double standard, threatening to cut off aid unless Hamas renounced violence, even though the group had maintained a year-long truce in the face of continued Israeli assassinations and land seizures. "America sees with only one eye and hears with only one ear," complained Salah Bardawil, Hamas's leader in the Palestinian Authority legislative council. "Now we are being asked to recognize Israel when it is annexing half of the West Bank behind the isolation wall."[45]

The divide between diplomatic rhetoric about the urgent need for a Palestinian state and diplomatic actions has never been more pronounced. It often seems that the endless rounds of meetings, seminars, and conferences by the Quartet, which always reaffirm support for the two-state solution, are designed to conceal the lack of political courage to confront the ways Israel has made this very solution impossible.

Supporters of Israeli policy have been extremely successful in their arguments that it is Palestinian violence that stands in the way of peaceful partition. This position, however, ignores several key facts. The immediate cause of the uprising that broke out in the occupied territories in September 2000 was Ariel Sharon's provocative visit to Muslim holy sites in Jerusalem accompanied by a thousand police. But the revolt was fueled by deeper Palestinian despair that years of negotiations and compromises had done nothing to rid them of the occupation or the ever-growing settlements, as well as by Israel's response, which was disproportionately brutal.[46] Young Palestinian militia leaders, having spent their whole lives under Israeli military rule, had reached the conclusion that armed struggle was once again the only way to make the cost of the occupation so high that Israel would have to end it.

Palestinian violence included various forms of resistance against the Israeli occupation, some legitimate, such as attacks that targetted Israeli tanks and troops in the Gaza Strip and West Bank, and some illegitimate, such as suicide bombings against noncombatant civilians. However, one cannot discount the truth that Palestinian violence occurs within the context of much greater and more pervasive Israeli violence. The claim that there is "no moral equivalency" between the Israeli army's killing of Palestinians and the deliberate killing of civilians by

Palestinian bombers rests on the assumption that Israel does all it can to avoid harm to civilians and that its violence is motivated purely by self-defense rather than the conquest of land.

Yet it is indisputable that the occupation and the settlements are maintained solely through the organized and systematic use of violence. The Israeli settlement project could not proceed without the use of violence. Imagine the success rate if settlers went knocking on doors asking Palestinians to kindly step out of their way. The scale of the violence that the settlements have entailed is breathtaking. Between 1993 and 2002, Israel forcibly confiscated 240 square kilometers of Palestinian land for settlements and their infrastructure (an area one and a third times *larger* than Washington, DC), destroyed or uprooted an estimated 1,034,852 trees, many of them fruit-bearing citrus and olive trees essential to the Palestinian economy and culture, and demolished over 4,000 Palestinian homes, affecting almost 100,000 people, according to a study by the Geneva-based Centre on Housing Rights and Evictions (COHRE).[47] From any moment you choose to measure, the ratio of unarmed Palestinian civilians killed by Israel is always far greater than the number of unarmed Israeli civilians killed by Palestinians.

While there is a mountain of testimony from Israeli, Palestinian, and international human rights groups and UN officials documenting Israel's violence against Palestinians, there is no denying that Israel has been successful in presenting Palestinian violence as the cause rather than the effect of its own practices. As long as Israel's actions continue, some Palestinians are always likely to fight back. Such resistance has rendered the settlement effort extremely costly to Israel, but it has been unable to stop the confiscation of Palestinian land, and therefore the attrition of any viable partition plan.

Within Palestinian society there is a constant debate about whether armed resistance has come at a moral and political price that is too high for Palestinians and has cost them much-needed allies. A visit to the occupied territories by Mahatma Gandhi's grandson, Arun Gandhi, in September 2004, sparked renewed discussion about the role of nonviolence in the Palestinian struggle for freedom. In a speech before the Palestinian Authority legislative council, Gandhi called upon 50,000 refugees to march back home en masse from their exile in Jordan, forcing the Israelis to choose between yielding to a wave of people power and gunning the marchers down in cold blood.

Palestinian Authority president Mahmoud Abbas gained credit in Western eyes by repeatedly criticizing his own people for "arming the Intifada" and has called for nonviolent resistance. This appeal has also been taken up in Israel. Yoel Esteron, former managing editor of *Ha'aretz*, wondered, "[W]hat would have happened if four years ago the Palestinians had chosen passive resistance?" Esteron opined: "It is worth it to them to choose Gandhi's way. And it is worth it to us. If the Palestinians stop committing suicide on our buses, this will be a more effective weapon than explosive belts. . . . Ostensibly, the key rests in the hands of the stronger side. Wrong. If Israel were to lay down its weapons, it would be forced to pick them up again after a few murderous terror attacks. . . . The key is in the Palestinians' hands."[48]

Such arguments assume that in response to nonviolent protest the Israeli government will change its policies and the

Israeli public will support Palestinian claims resulting in real change. But much of the broad-based popular intifada of 1987 to 1993 was characterized by peaceful mass protests, strikes, and civil disobedience, including the refusal to pay taxes imposed by the occupation. The first Intifada certainly forced Israelis to realize that they could not rule indefinitely over millions of disenfranchised Palestinians, but Israel met this challenge not by laying down its arms or slowing the construction of new settlements, but with escalating violence and more settlements. It was this experience that led many Palestinians to believe that nonviolence was futile and that Israeli fire could only be fought with more fire.

One of the things that the violence-obsessed media coverage conceals is that nonviolence is and has always been integral to Palestinian resistance. The word for it in Arabic is *sumud*—steadfastness. When Israeli walls and roadblocks prevent people from moving, and yet children and old women, workers, students, mothers each day, every day climb hills and mountains to get where they need to go, that is *sumud*. When Israeli occupation forces uproot trees and farmers replant them, that is *sumud*. When Israel uses every administrative and legalistic means to force Palestinian Jerusalemites to leave the city for good, but instead they stay, even if it means being painfully separated from family members in the West Bank, that is *sumud*. Millions of Palestinians practice nonviolence every day, yet this is ignored by the media and by politicians and is totally invisible to the vast majority of Israelis.

During the Oslo years, a Hamas bombing was far more likely to bring the region's leaders rushing to Sharm al-Sheikh for a summit than the countless protests, strikes, and sit-ins against the growing settlements or in support of thousands of prisoners. More recently, Palestinian villages like Biddu and Bil'in that lie in the path of the separation wall have mounted grassroots nonviolent campaigns to try to save their land, only to be met with bullets. Many Palestinians, as well as some international campaigners like Rachel Corrie and Tom Hurndall, have been killed by the Israeli army during such peaceful, unarmed actions.

The "oft-heard accusation that the Palestinians have not chosen civil revolt instead of violence," observed *Ha'aretz* columnist Gideon Levy, "ignores the fact that they always encounter a violent reaction" from Israel no matter what the form of protest.[49] Now, with the restrictions on Palestinian movement, and the high risks of undertaking nonviolent resistance, the chances of such campaigns gaining enough momentum to stop the settlement drive and force an Israeli withdrawal remain negligible.

At the heart of the rarely questioned nostrum that peace will come through the creation of a Palestinian state alongside Israel lies an assumption that the country can be partitioned in a way that is practical and acceptable to a majority on both sides. Some sort of viable partition exists out there, according to this logic, ready to be seized if Israeli and Palestinian leaders are sufficiently courageous and defeat their respective extremists, who are seen as the key obstacles to reaching the desired goal. This idea, which tends to dominate political commentary, avoids the central question of whether it is really possible to separate two deeply intertwined populations, and whether they really want what separation would entail. Ongoing diplomatic efforts concentrate exclusively on whatever latest incident has derailed the train from its journey to the ever-close but ever-unreachable destination of a mutually acceptable division of the land.

But both Israeli and Palestinian public opinion reveals how illusory this idea is. In poll after poll, 60 to 70 percent of Israelis consistently say that they favor the creation of a Palestinian state and the dismantling of West Bank settlements if only there were a suitable Palestinian partner with whom to work. Yet Israelis keep electing leaders who build ever more settlements. What explains this puzzling inconsistency? A 2005 survey carried out by Israel's Dahaf Institute on behalf of the Palestinian Center for Israel Studies suggests an answer: It found that only 34 percent of Israeli Jews would support a full withdrawal to the 1967 border, while 65 percent opposed it. The reason for the discrepancy in the polls is that most do not specify the boundaries of this Palestinian state nor assert that all or even most of the settlements would have to be removed.[50] When most Israeli Jews speak of settlements, they think of distant outposts established by religious zealots. They often exclude from their definition the largest and most populous colonies like Ma'ale Adumim, Gilo, and Gush Etzion, which they simply view as "neighborhoods" or suburbs of Jerusalem. Yet these are the very settlements that have destroyed the contiguity of the West Bank and cut Palestinians off from Jerusalem and from each other. According to Dr. Assad Ghanem, the

Palestinian researcher who commissioned the study, "Only a minority of Israelis are willing to accept the state that the Palestinians are talking about, and this fact was only revealed because we formulated the survey questions from our own standpoint rather than from the standpoint of Jewish Israeli pollsters." Israeli journalist Amira Hass observed that, in the 1990s, as settlements continued to expand,

> the number of Israelis who had a vested interest in the settlements grew dramatically. In the '70s and '80s the numbers were very small and that's why Peace Now could come out with a slogan that was accepted that said that peace is incompatible with settlements. The 1990s were the opposite. . . . You have at least one more million Israelis [who] have family in settlements. The settlements are something natural. They go and visit and they drive on roads; they have no idea . . . on which land the roads were built. For them it's as natural as the sunrise. You have an enormous number of soldiers who defend these settlers so they grow their affinity with those settlers. . . . You have an unknown number of people who are working in the intelligence because you also have to defend these settlements. They all have family; all these people know about the settlements and grow to accept it as a natural thing. You have teachers, you have doctors, you have all sorts of ministry employees, you have infrastructure workers, contractors, construction workers. So there is a whole mass of Israelis which in the years of the so-called peace process were growing more and more attached to the settlements.[51]

Israelis and most American Jews polled like the idea of a Palestinian state, but not if it means actually giving up real control over much of the occupied territories.

Part of the conventional wisdom of the peace process has been that Palestinians can be forced to accept the large settlement blocs as a fait accompli, thus indulging the Israeli unwillingness to give them up. But fewer than 4 percent of Palestinians in the occupied territories accept Israeli annexation of the large settlements, indicating that there is little readiness on either side to agree on a partition line of any kind.[52] Even the most forthcoming Israeli peace plans envisage removing no more than about 20 percent of the settlers in the West Bank and fall far short of minimum Palestinian expectations. Palestinians through years of peace talks have watched as Israel has used its superior power to take ever more of the land. They have tried all the possible approaches available to the weaker side: armed struggle, nonviolent resistance, and appeals for international intervention. That the two sides might reach voluntary agreement is unlikely, to say the least, and there seems to be no constellation of internal or external forces that will push Israel out of the West Bank against its will.

So where does that leave the two-state solution? The stark reality is that partition, despite the copious lip-service it receives, has always been hard to attain; today in the face of Israel's takeover of what is left of Palestinian land and the international refusal to confront it, partition is unachievable.

CHAPTER TWO

"The State of Israel
Is Coming to an End"

In 1996, on my first visit to Jerusalem, I saw for myself the devastating effects of Mayor Ehud Olmert's drive to Judaize the eastern part of the city at the expense of Palestinians. The landscape of misery and rubble—the remains of demolished Palestinian houses—so appalled me that I was driven on a fool's errand to the Israeli city hall in Jerusalem to confront the mayor with the names of those Palestinians he had made homeless. I never got past the angry receptionist, and Olmert, a stalwart of the nationalist right, remained committed to securing "Greater Israel" through settlement. As two-term mayor of Jerusalem, he contributed mightily to advance the expansionist cause.

Hence the profound shock Israelis felt some eight years later when Olmert, now Sharon's deputy prime minister, pronounced himself in favor of withdrawal from parts of the occupied territories. His logic was clear: "We are approaching the point where more and more Palestinians will say, 'There is no place for two states between the Jordan and the sea. All we want is the right to vote.' The day they get it, we will lose everything." Warning that Israel could not remain both a Jewish state and a democracy if it held all the territories, Olmert added, "I shudder to think that liberal Jewish organizations that shouldered the burden of struggle against apartheid in South Africa will lead the struggle against us."[1] One prominent Israeli journalist quipped that the effect of Olmert's change of heart was more surprising than "if Dick Cheney came out for socialism."[2] Stunning though it was, Olmert's conversion was only a trial balloon for Sharon and the opening volley in a gambit to enlist Israelis in a new campaign called "disengagement." This opening volley led directly to Sharon's break with the Likud to establish, along with senior Labor politicians including Shimon Peres, Kadima, a party that carried the banner for a new political consensus.

To most commentators a seismic shift was under way in Israeli politics, one that might at last herald a two-state solution. However this shift was hardly prompted by the wish for a viable, independent Palestinian state alongside Israel. Rather, the embrace of "disengagement" or "unilateral separation" from the Palestinian population of the occupied territories was an unambiguous response to the reality that the "demographic time bomb," so threatening to Israeli leaders, was about to go off. The result of "disengagement," if implemented along Israeli lines, would in fact be to shred what remained of a viable Palestinian state.

In August 2005, for the first time since Israel was established, Jews no longer formed an absolute majority in the territory they controlled. Israel's Central Bureau of Statistics counted 5.26 million Jews living in Israel-Palestine and, combined with figures from the Palestinian Central Bureau of Statistics, there were 5.62 million non-Jews. Within Israel's 1967 borders there were just under 5 million Jews alongside 1.35 million Palestinians, 185,000 foreign workers, and 290,000 classified as "other." In the West Bank, there were 400,000 Jewish settlers and 2.4 million Palestinians, and another 1.4 million Palestinians in the Gaza Strip. Thus in Israel, the West Bank, and Gaza Strip combined, the Jewish and Palestinian populations are statistically equal, with Jews comprising just under half the total population. Professor Arnon Soffer, chair of geostrategic studies at the University of Haifa, predicts that by 2020 there will be 6.3 million Jews and 8.8 million Palestinians due to the high Palestinian birth rate.[3] Sergio Della Pergola, a demographer at the Hebrew University, notes that even using the lowest possible credible estimates for the Palestinian population in the occupied territories, the trends are "incontestable": Within a few years Palestinians will form a clear majority.[4]

Israel's pullout from the Gaza Strip allowed it to "subtract" the 1.4 million Palestinians who live there and claim therefore that the overall Jewish majority is back up to about 57 percent. Even if we agree to exclude the Palestinians in Gaza, the disengagement provides only short-term respite. Soffer warns that, excluding Palestinians in Gaza, on the basis of current trends the balance between Jews and Palestinians will be back to 50–50 within two decades.[5]

Israel's current tactic of unilateral disengagement or separation is an attempt to answer this demographic dilemma. It is an effort to define boundaries for the state that assure a Jewish majority, but doesn't involve genuinely giving up control of the occupied territories; the withdrawal from Gaza, with Israel maintaining its grip on the borders and its right to military action, demonstrates this clearly. This supposedly new turn is in fact entirely consistent with policies in place for decades, despite what appears to be a dramatic change in Israeli priorities. Soffer has been one of the most prominent prophets of demographic doom, though he exaggerates somewhat when he says Israelis have ignored the issue for many years. In fact, fear of the "demographic threat" from Palestinians has been pervasive, lying at the core of Jewish approaches to the conflict since the birth of the Zionist movement. The initial demographic conundrum, so clearly seen by the Peel Commission in 1937, was alleviated in 1948 through the expulsion and flight of the vast majority of Palestinians from what became the state of Israel. Between 1948 and 1967, as Jews comprised the overwhelming majority within Israel's borders the demographic problem, from Israel's perspective, appeared to be solved. However, Israel's occupation of East Jerusalem, the West Bank, and the Gaza Strip meant also ruling over these areas' Palestinian inhabitants. Now Israelis had to grapple with what to do with all those people living on land that Israel began to settle and wanted to keep.

The Labor Party, which dominated Israel's government until the late 1970s, hit upon the idea of separating control of the land from responsibility for the people. In 1976, Yigal Allon, a key figure in Israeli military and Labor Party history who served in several senior cabinet posts, articulated a plan under which Israel would annex Jerusalem and its environs as well as roughly half the occupied West Bank, including the entire Jordan Valley.⁶ The plan provided the security rationale for the establishment, under Labor governments, of dozens of Israeli settlements in the occupied West Bank to "create facts" in the areas Allon envisaged annexing.

While pursuing the Allon plan on the ground, Labor Party leaders like Shimon Peres—who vocally supported the settlements—searched for solutions that would allow Israel to dump political responsibility for the Palestinians even as it consolidated its control of the land. Allon, as hostile as most Israelis were at that time to the notion of indigenous Palestinian national identity, proposed allowing Jordan to govern the Palestinians in day-to-day affairs, subject to overall Israeli control. Although never acceptable to more than a handful of Palestinians, the "Jordanian option" attracted Israeli leaders because it seemed to offer a way to allow them to keep the newly conquered land, prevent the emergence of a Palestinian state ruled by the dominant PLO, and resolve the political conflict all at the same time. With the Palestinians under occupation still largely docile and providing a limitless source of cheap labor to the Israeli economy, a solution did not seem urgent.

For the first two decades of the occupation, according to Azmi Bishara, a Palestinian citizen of Israel and member of the Knesset, Israel's policy in the occupied territories prior to the first Intifada "boiled down to two 'Nos'—no withdrawal and no annexation." This allowed Israel to exploit the land and resources without confronting the dilemma of granting political rights to the people who lived on it. In 1987 the first "intifada came along and added another 'No,'" says Bishara, "no withdrawal, no annexation, but no status quo."[7] The intifada posed a major challenge particularly to the Israeli Labor party, largely the parliamentary home of Israel's left, which had concluded that outright opposition to any accommodation with the Palestinians was untenable. Labor politicians, who wished to project an image of Israel in the mold of a benign Western European–style social democracy, were embarrassed by international criticism of the harsh response to Palestinian protests, a response that revealed the true face of military rule. At the same time, Labor's message became increasingly defined by demographic fear-mongering. Peres led Labor into the 1988 elections warning of the dangers of the growing Palestinian population, promising, "[W]e shall rid ourselves of areas densely populated by Arabs."[8] Other Labor politicians sought to scare voters with the fact that "in Israel and the territories together, there are more Arabs than Jews in kindergarten and first grade."[9] With the pressure of the intifada and demographic reality breathing down their necks, Labor leaders such as Peres and Yitzhak Rabin began to hint that they might support some form of a Palestinian state, but without ever referring to specific borders.

The Israeli right, while not oblivious to the demographic "problem," fretted about it less than the left, preferring a tactic of stretching out political processes to buy time for the settlement effort. Confident in its ability to bring about a demographic transformation, which, it hoped, would seal Israel's claim to the occupied territories, the right absolutely rejected a Palestinian state. When Likud leader Menachem Begin assumed power in 1977, he vowed that Israel would never give up its hold on "Judea and

Samaria" and Gaza, but resisted calls from his supporters to annex the territories outright. Begin knew that incorporation of the large Palestinian population would be problematic—Israel wouldn't give them political rights and equal citizenship, but nor could it rule perpetually by force. In the 1979 Camp David Accords with Egypt, Begin contemplated limited "personal" autonomy for the Palestinians, specifically ruling out anything that smacked of territorial sovereignty or self-determination. The Likud's foot-dragging approach was typified by Begin's successor, Yitzhak Shamir, who led Israel into the 1991 Madrid Peace Conference under intense pressure from George H. W. Bush's administration. After Shamir left office, he revealed that he "would have conducted negotiations on autonomy for 10 years and in the meantime we would have reached half a million people [Jews] in the West Bank."[10]

Likud's stalling was too crude to succeed indefinitely, especially in the face of the political reality evolving on the Palestinian front. Taken by surprise by the intifada—a phenomenon initiated and led by a new generation within the occupied territories—Yasser Arafat, leader of the PLO in exile and marginalized in distant Tunis, quickly moved to capitalize on the uprising while at the same time neutralizing it as a threat to the primacy of senior PLO incumbents. Contact with Israeli and American Jewish activists encouraged Arafat to believe that moderation on his part—full acceptance of Israel's "right to exist" and renunciation of "terrorism"—would lead to his acceptance as a peace partner and ultimately to the creation of a Palestinian state.

On November 15, 1988, the PLO's legislative body, the Palestinian National Council (PNC), met in Algiers and formally adopted the two-state solution, announcing its acceptance of the partition of Palestine and all other UN resolutions that served as the basis for the two-state concept. This move represented a gut-wrenching and difficult shift in Palestinian thinking that had taken decades to evolve. It meant legitimizing the Israeli state on the 78 percent of Palestine on which it was established in 1948, and settling for statehood on just 22 percent of the country—East Jerusalem, the West Bank, and Gaza Strip. Most Palestinians were prepared to accept this enormous compromise, while those opposed to the two-state solution were relegated to the political wilderness. At Algiers, the PNC symbolically declared the independence of the "State of Palestine" in the occupied territories although it in fact controlled no land. This "state" was then formally recognized by dozens of countries, though not by the United States or most of Western Europe.

Then in 1992, the Israeli Labor Party, fully back in power for the first time since 1977, met this growing challenge with a formula that involved neither real withdrawal from occupied territory nor genuine Palestinian independence but a sufficient imitation of both to defuse the pressure. To much of the world, the Oslo Accords officially signed on the White House lawn in September 1993 looked like an amazing breakthrough. Many Palestinians were euphoric, believing at last that their dream to be rid of the occupation was about to come true. Khaled, who grew up in the West Bank town of Jericho and now lives in Chicago, remembers that on hearing news of the agreement some young Palestinians rushed out to throw what they thought would be the very last stones at Israeli occupation forces. Others offered the Israeli soldiers flowers.

But the disappointment was proportionately bitter as Oslo turned out to be no more than a continuation of Israel's effort to keep control of the land while delegating day-to-day responsibility for the Palestinians who lived in it. Oslo, with its appearance of self-determination, blurred the outright inequities and gross power imbalance providing the illusion of two roughly equal parties on their way to resolving a conflict. Shimon Peres grasped that to achieve this feat, in Israeli eyes, Arafat would need to undergo a transformation "from the most hated gentleman in this country . . . with an array of very strange ideas, into a partner that we can sit with." He needed to become "acceptable to our people—maybe not beloved but at least accepted."[11] This was a tall order, because, as Peres saw it, Arafat did not look "terribly attractive," his speeches were "very revolting," he represented "everything that the Israeli people didn't like," and then there were "his demands on Jerusalem." Peres concluded, "[H]e makes our lives so complicated."[12] (Nominally, Arafat's demand regarding Jerusalem was that Israel withdraw from the eastern part occupied in 1967, in accordance with international law, so that it could become the Palestinian capital.)

Nevertheless, Peres urged Prime Minister Yitzhak Rabin to sign the agreement, telling him, "Why should we keep [Arafat] in Tunisia, making troubles from there? Let him come to the heart of the troubles. Let him be on the spot, in Gaza." Peres calculated—accurately—that Arafat would eagerly trade the opportunity to play the assigned role of "partner" for concessions on every issue of substance, including the Jewish settlements, the nature and boundaries of a Palestinian state, Jerusalem, the status of Palestinian prisoners held by Israel, and the fate of the refugees exiled in the wars of 1947–49 and 1967.[13] According to one Israeli negotiator, the Peres-Rabin camp thought it was worth making a deal with Arafat because there was "no one else" in a position to "agree to autonomy with interim arrangements" and "pursue terrorists, apprehend them, put them in jail—without getting even . . . minimum requirements" from Israel.[14] Oslo was "an exercise in make-believe," according to Shlomo Ben-Ami, a former Israeli foreign minister deeply involved in the peace process, creating drastically "different expectations" among the parties. The ambiguities in the terms and the fact that the agreement included no mention of Palestinian "self-determination" made it easier to clinch the deal in the short term, explained Ben-Ami, but only delayed the day when negotiators would confront the two sides' irreconcilable expectations. Rabin, Ben-Ami added, "never thought this will end in a full-fledged Palestinian state."[15]

To this day Palestinians wonder why Arafat agreed to sign the various Oslo agreements. Whatever the reasons, he paid in advance with full recognition of Israel while receiving no reciprocal promise of a full withdrawal from the occupied territories or acknowledgment of a Palestinian right to independence. The Oslo accords can be summed up as the fulfillment of Peres's wishes: a partner molded to suit Israel's liking and an endless process to avoid central facts of the conflict—Jerusalem, the settlements, refugees—that made things so "complicated." As Palestinians like Khaled soon discovered, the grim reality was that Oslo transformed the crude occupation into something more insidious, hiding it behind a PLO facade.

Ultimately, the series of accords signed between 1993 and 1995 created a new set of complications. The agreements called for the creation of a Palestinian Authority (P.A.) to exercise control over Palestinians living in the West Bank and Gaza Strip, but not over the territory and its borders. In the West Bank, the territory was divided into three areas, A, B, and C. Area A covered the major cities, including Ramallah, Bethlehem, Nablus, and Jericho but not Jerusalem, and was ostensibly under full security control of the P.A., but it comprised initially just 3 percent of the land and never exceeded 18 percent. Area B, a quarter of the land, was designated under Israeli "security" control but Palestinian "civil" control. In almost three-quarters of the West Bank, Area C, and on the borders, Israel remained in full control, as evidenced by the P.A.'s inability to afford any protection to Palestinians whose land was seized for settlement construction. Oslo raised symbols of sovereignty and then made a mockery of them. One example, described by Israeli negotiator Uri Savir, involved the passage of Palestinians returning to the West Bank from neighboring Jordan:

A Palestinian stamps their passport [*sic*]. Behind the Palestinian there is tinted glass. Behind that, an Israeli. The Palestinian puts the documents in a box. They go to the Israeli, who has a computer. He can send them back, with questions. The Palestinian asks them. Only if the person is suspect does he go into a back room to be interrogated. There was a three-day discussion as to whether the glass should be tinted or opaque. I think we decided dark-tinted.[16]

Israel had transferred responsibility but without power or independence and Palestinians came increasingly to see the P.A. not as a vehicle for liberation but as a proxy force designed to relieve Israel of the various costs of enforcing the occupation itself. Arafat had not liberated his people from occupation but joined them under it.

The conventional wisdom is that the Oslo process failed because of violence, immutable hatred, "extremism on both sides," or because Rabin was assassinated in November 1995, leading in 1996 to the election of a hard-line government under Benjamin Netanyahu. But these explanations ignore the effect of Israel's drive for land and control, which ran directly counter to the possibility of creating a Palestinian state. Defenders of Israel's actions argue that the PLO too did not follow the letter of the agreements. Israel constantly complained that the P.A. hired more police officers than the agreements allowed, and was never satisfied that the P.A. arrested enough of the people on the wanted lists Israel drew up. But there is no evidence that the acceleration of the Israeli settlements was designed as retaliation for such transgressions. It is not credible that a society would invest billions of dollars in roads and housing that it truly intended to give up.

If Israel conceded little at Oslo, it gained unprecedented international prestige and concrete benefits from the deal. Then–finance minister Avraham Shochat observed that "[i]n 1992, Israel attracted some $140 million in foreign investments." In 1996, investments had increased by twenty-fold to $3 billion. Israel's economy grew by a soaring 6 percent yearly in the four years after the agreements were signed. "Oslo had an extraordinary effect on our status in the world," Shochat noted. "The fact that we signed an agreement and embarked on a peace process gave Israel a legitimacy that it had never before possessed."[17] Diplomats and businessmen from Arab states in North Africa and the Persian Gulf, and other Muslim states like Indonesia and Malaysia, all lined up to do business with the Jewish state.[18]

The lasting legacy of the Oslo process is that far from advancing the two-state solution, it in fact laid the groundwork for the fragmentation of the occupied territories—which has reached new extremes with the construction of the separation wall—and legitimized the idea that the primary role of any Palestinian government is not to protect its citizens from the occupation but to protect the occupation and the settlers from their Palestinian subjects.

Of all the myths in the recent history of the Palestinian-Israeli conflict the most enduring is that the Camp David summit of 2000, chaired by President Clinton, concluded with Arafat's rejection of a generous offer from Prime Minister Ehud Barak that could have ended the hostilities once and for all. Many commentators unquestioningly parrot specific percentages of the West Bank from which Israel ostensibly "offered" to withdraw, ranging from 90 to 97 percent. Shimon Peres even claimed that "Prime Minister Barak has actually offered hundred percent [*sic*] of the West Bank and Gaza and part of Jerusalem. . . . It is very hard for the Israelis to understand why did actually the Palestinians reject it."[19] Influential *New York Times* columnist Thomas Friedman called the Palestinians "insane" for rebuffing Israel's alleged generosity.[20] This myth did not emerge just because of the American media's well-documented tendency to adopt Israel's interpretation on most key issues.[21] Rather, President Clinton and the Israeli government made a calculated decision and embarked on an orchestrated media campaign to blame the Palestinians generally and Arafat personally for the summit's failure.[22]

A year after the summit, Robert Malley, Clinton's special assistant for Arab-Israeli affairs and a key negotiator at Camp David, struck a blow at the myth. Malley wrote:

Many have come to believe that the Palestinians' rejection of the Camp David ideas exposed an underlying rejection of Israel's right to exist. But consider the facts: The Palestinians were arguing for the creation of a Palestinian state based on the June 4, 1967, borders, living alongside Israel. They accepted the notion of Israeli annexation of West Bank territory to accommodate settlement blocs. They accepted the principle of Israeli sovereignty over the Jewish neighborhoods of East Jerusalem—neighborhoods that were not part of Israel before the Six Day War in

1967. And, while they insisted on recognition of the refugees' right of return, they agreed that it should be implemented in a manner that protected Israel's demographic and security interests by limiting the number of returnees. No other Arab party that has negotiated with Israel—not Anwar el-Sadat's Egypt, not King Hussein's Jordan, let alone Hafez al-Assad's Syria—ever came close to even considering such compromises.[23]

Malley concluded that "[i]f peace is to be achieved, the parties cannot afford to tolerate the growing acceptance of these myths as reality." Malley's account has been amplified in a meticulous history of the Camp David summit by Clayton Swisher, a former U.S. marine reservist and federal criminal investigator.[24] Swisher interviewed virtually all of the participants in the summit from the U.S., Israeli, and Palestinian sides as well as officials from the governments of Syria, Saudi Arabia, Egypt, and Sweden who had direct participation in events leading up to the summit.

What then did the Palestinian negotiators reject of Barak's "generous offer"? As far as territory is concerned, the Israelis presented only one map at Camp David, and it contained nothing new; they had presented the same map to Palestinian negotiators months previously and the Palestinians had rejected it.[25] It depicted a Palestinian "state" in 76.6 percent of the West Bank, broken into pieces, with all the major settlements remaining in place under Israeli sovereignty. Israel would annex 13.3 percent outright and continue to occupy the remaining 10.1 percent for a period of up to thirty years, during which time there would be no restriction on Israel continuing to build settlements and infrastructure.[26]

It should be noted that even before these percentages were calculated, the Israelis already subtracted East Jerusalem and the territorial waters of the Dead Sea, so, in fact, the 76 percent offer was based not on 100 percent of the occupied territories, but only on those parts that Israel was prepared to discuss. Leaving aside the disjointed nature of this "state," its territory would amount to just 16 percent of historic Palestine, a compromise on the compromise that no Palestinian leader could make. Barak refused to relinquish Israel's claim to sovereignty over the Muslim holy places in Jerusalem (the Haram al-Sharif), but was prepared to offer the Palestinians "functional" control. It is not true, as many have claimed, that the Palestinians failed to make a counteroffer: In response to Israel's map, the Palestinian team presented its own map that allowed 30 to 35 percent of the settlers to remain on 2.5 percent of the West Bank, which Israel could annex. The Israelis rejected this outright and came back with a counterproposal in which they increased their offer from 76.6 percent to 77.2 percent and insisted that at least 80 percent of the settlers remain in place.[27] A senior Clinton adviser commented that the Israelis were attempting to execute a "land grab."[28] Israel also insisted on permanent control of Palestinian airspace and a long list of onerous "security" arrangements that would rob the Palestinian state of any real independence from Israel and introduce enormous opportunities for delay and backsliding as had happened with the Oslo Accords. Israel's proposals at Camp David barely deviated from the basic premises of the 1976 Allon plan.

The legacy of the failed Camp David summit cannot be underestimated. To Palestinians, it demonstrated that even with the highest level of U.S. involvement, no Israeli government would sign a peace agreement if it meant giving up more than a token number of settlements and any real control in the West Bank. To Israelis, Camp David gave birth to an enduring myth, neatly encapsulated by left-wing novelist Amos Oz, who wrote:

> Ehud Barak went a very long way towards Palestinians, even before the beginning of the Camp David summit; longer than any of his predecessors ever dreamt to go; longer than any other Israeli prime minister is likely to go. On the way to Camp David, Barak's proclaimed stance was so dovish that it made him lose his parliamentary majority, his coalition government, even some of his constituency. Nevertheless, while shedding wings and body and tail on the way, he carried on like a flying cockpit, he carried on. Seemingly Yasser Arafat did not go such a long and lonely way towards the Israelis. Perhaps he could not, or lacked the fierce devotion to making peace.[29]

After Camp David, the belief took hold in Israel that there was no possibility of a negotiated two-state settlement with the Palestinians and that the state was therefore justified in taking whatever unilateral action it deemed necessary. When the Labor Party unveiled its 2006 platform reaffirming its determination to annex the large settlement blocs, a senior party official admitted that "the differences between Labor and Kadima are not in the contents but in the possibility of carrying them out."[30] Labor still believed that Palestinians could be forced to capitulate in "negotiations," while Sharon and his allies believed in a straightforward land-grab under the pretext that there is no Palestinian "partner." Each approach is in its way a direct descendant of Oslo, and neither offers a real path out of Israel's demographic dead end.

Those Israelis who insist that a negotiated partition is still possible and merely awaits the emergence of responsible leaders have lined up behind the Geneva Initiative, perhaps the best-known and most influential example of this stream of thought. A project of Israel's former justice minister Yossi Beilin and Yasir Abed Rabbo, former culture minister in the Palestinian Authority, the initiative was launched at a star-studded ceremony presided over by actor Richard Dreyfuss in December 2003. The creators of this unofficial peace plan have sold it as a breakthrough that proves a two-state solution remains viable. In reality, the clear advances in the plan, vague as it is, appear to be minimal—a little less land annexation and fewer settlers remaining in place—while its essence carried over the basic tenets of Camp David: the permanence of settlements and the preservation of an effective Israeli veto on real Palestinian independence.

The vision of a peaceful division of the land achieved through discussion remains attractive, which perhaps explains why the Geneva Initiative gained endorsements from newspapers, columnists, celebrities, and politicians around the world. Beilin, the chief architect of the Oslo Accords together with Peres, and the main force behind the Geneva Initiative, was concerned chiefly with preserving a Jewish majority in an internationally recognized Israel while refusing to withdraw from most of the West Bank settlements and Jerusalem. Beilin has opposed unilateral Israeli withdrawal because, he argued, only full unilateral withdrawal—i.e. to the 1967 borders—would "gain legitimization—world-wide and regional," thus making it necessary to "give up all the settlements and relinquish the territory in Jerusalem taken over in the Six-Day War."[31] Partial unilateral withdrawal allowing Israel to keep its war gains might be feasible, but, Beilin warned, would be considered illegitimate in the eyes of the world and remain a continuing source of conflict. His ideal, thus, was a partial withdrawal with Palestinian agreement, an ideal that the Geneva Initiative, and Oslo and Camp David before it, sought to achieve.

Beilin and Abed Rabbo claimed that their document resolved "all the major differences between the parties, including security arrangements, the shape of permanent borders, the status of Jerusalem, the future of West Bank settlements, the rights of refugees, and access to holy places."[32] The reality was that the terms of the plan did not deviate significantly from the approach taken at Camp David on all the key issues, including borders, settlements, Jerusalem, and refugee rights. The Geneva Initiative would leave the vast majority of the settlements in place and give Israel a veto on the return of Palestinian refugees to homes inside Israel.

Demilitarized, the Palestinian state would have severe limits to its sovereignty. Its external borders would remain under "unseen" Israeli control for five years, and then under the indefinite control of a "Multinational Force" that could not be modified or withdrawn without Israel's consent. Israel would keep military forces in the Jordan Valley for an initial but renewable three years and be allowed to keep "early warning stations" inside the Palestinian state permanently. Israeli military personnel and equipment would be withdrawn from the Palestinian state "except as otherwise agreed," in a document referred to throughout the accord as "Annex X." The problem is that Annex X, to which many other significant details about Israeli rights to use Palestinian airspace, electromagnetic spectrum, and territory for military purposes are relegated, does not actually exist; its terms were never set by the Geneva Initiative participants. The provisions about a symbolic return of refugees to within the 1967 borders are designed entirely to preserve a Jewish majority for as long as possible. For Jerusalem, the initiative adopts the idea set out by President Clinton in December 2000 that "Arab neighborhoods" in Jerusalem should be under Palestinian sovereignty, while "Jewish neighborhoods" should be under Israeli sovereignty. This sounds like the epitome of fairness on its face, but "Jewish neighborhood" is a euphemism for settlements built on land forcibly expropriated from Palestinian owners. If this presentation seems overly negative, consider how retired general Amram Mitzna, former Labor Party leader and one of the Geneva Initiative authors, presented it to the Israeli public:

For the first time in history, the Palestinians explicitly and officially recognized the state of Israel as the state of the

Jewish people forever. They gave up the right of return to
the state of Israel and a solid, stable Jewish majority was
guaranteed. The Western Wall, the Jewish Quarter, and
David's Tower will all remain in our hands. The suffo-
cating ring was lifted from over Jerusalem and the entire
ring of settlements around it—Givat Ze'ev, old and new
Givon, Ma'ale Adumim, Gush Etzion, Neve Yaacov, Pis-
gat Ze'ev, French Hill, Ramot, Gilo, and Armon Hanatziv
will be part of the expanded city, forever. None of the settlers in those areas will have to leave their homes.[33]

The places mentioned by Mitzna include almost 170,000
settlers and account for the largest land expropriations in the
most densely populated Palestinian areas in the West Bank. But
they are not the only settlements that the Geneva Initiative
would allow Israel to keep. On the publicity maps on the
Geneva Initiative's English Web site, the proposed annexations
appear minimal because the maps are at such a low resolution.[34]
Much more detailed maps, available only at the Geneva Initiative's Hebrew Web site (there does not appear to be an Arabic
Web site), show how devastating the initiative would really be
to Palestinians on the ground.[35] To take one example, the Palestinian city of Qalqilya in the northwest of the West Bank is
sandwiched between the 1967 border with Israel on the west
and north and the settlement of Alfe Menashe (population
5,000) on the east. Under the Geneva Initiative, Israel would
keep this settlement and annex a wide swath of territory around
it and a corridor linking it to Israel. This mushroom-shaped
land grab would completely encircle Qalqilya from the south,

severely limiting the growth potential for the city and its neighboring villages (population 60,000). The corridor connecting the settlement to Israel does even more damage by bisecting two Palestinian villages, cutting them off from each other and cutting many more Palestinians off from Qalqilya.

In his book *The Path to Geneva,* Beilin recalled the "negotiation" in which this came about: "[T]he most important decision made regarding territorial issues was the annexation of the Alfe Menashe settlement to Israel in return for the concession of Efrat," a settlement near Bethlehem.[36] Beilin has a very strange idea of give and take, when *both* Alfe Menashe and Efrat are built on occupied land seized from Palestinians. Frantz Fanon's description of decolonization in Africa was never more apt: "What was wrested by bombardments is reconverted into the results of free negotiations."[37] The Geneva Initiative is nominally "fair" in that land annexed in one place is compensated somewhere else on a one-for-one basis. But exchanging sand dunes south of Gaza or barren hills west of Hebron—as Geneva proposes—for neighborhoods of Jerusalem is as absurd as saying that Manhattan or the heart of Paris could be exchanged for an equally sized piece of the Nevada desert. In none of the "exchanges" contained in the Geneva plan do Palestinians receive anything remotely comparable to what they would give up.

The Geneva Initiative benefited from a big-budget promotional campaign that created the impression, internationally, at least, that it represents a broad spectrum of Israeli and Palestinian public opinion. To the extent that there is a general consensus in favor of a two-state solution, it does. But it did not succeed in breaking the basic impasse. Under the tutelage of Beilin, Abed Rabbo established the Palestinian Peace Coalition (PPC), an organization dedicated to promoting "separation in a two-state solution" among Palestinians, working in close cooperation with Beilin's own Israeli Peace Coalition. Yet efforts to win support for the Geneva Initiative among Palestinians foundered on the Israeli participants' insistence on keeping most of the settlers in place and its failure to resolve the refugee issue in an acceptable manner. Two prominent figures, Qadoura Fares, a Fatah legislator and sometime Palestinian Authority minister, and Muhammad Hourani, a well-known peace activist, volunteered to join the PPC and endorse the Geneva Initiative. "Their involvement was welcome," Beilin recalls, but eventually had to be rejected because "they demanded that Israel give up the settlement of Ma'ale Adumim or Givat Ze'ev in order to create space for the development of East Jerusalem, and that additional territory be transferred to establish a large settlement for Palestinian refugees. We explained that although their involvement was very important to us, we would not be able to meet these demands."[38] This intransigence was not lost on Palestinians, despite the hype around Geneva. At Gaza City's Rashad Shawa Cultural Center, the Palestinian Legislative Council speaker was one among many public figures to condemn the agreement at a "popular conference in defense of the right of return and for confronting the dangers of the Geneva Accord." Many similar rallies were held at universities and refugee camps. Al-Haq, the renowned human rights organization, published a detailed legal commentary that concluded that the initiative's provisions on settlements and refugees violate fundamental principles of international human rights and humanitarian law.[39]

Among Israelis and Zionists, reaction to the Geneva Initiative was more divided. Right-wingers predictably saw its territorial component as caving in to Palestinians, but even the left expressed reservations about the extent of the initiative's concessions. Overall, it enjoyed the support of only one-quarter of Israeli Jews, while 54 percent opposed it, according to one study by the widely respected Tami Steinmetz Center for Peace Research at Tel Aviv University.[40] Beilin found little backing for the plan in the Labor Party, which he had left in late 2002 after a poor showing in primary elections, to join the tiny left-wing Meretz Party.

Although the Geneva Initiative made little headway among Israelis or Palestinians, it and similar plans remain very popular among peace activists around the world, particularly liberal American Zionist groups. One Voice, a plan endorsed by actors Brad Pitt, Danny DeVito, and Jason Alexander, gained significant support from major foundations to carry out promotional campaigns on U.S. campuses. Another virtual peace effort making the rounds, called People's Voice, is based on the Geneva-like ideas of academic and former Palestinian Authority Jerusalem spokesman Sari Nusseibeh and former Israeli intelligence chief Ami Ayalon. What all these approaches have in common and the way they differ from the unilateral approach is not that they are significantly more forthcoming to Palestinians, but rather that they seek Palestinian endorsement of Israel's annexation of territory and of its refusal to readmit Palestinian refugees to their country. In an apt comment made during the Oslo negotiations, Beilin had argued that the challenge for reaching an agreement on Jerusalem "is what to call the status quo, because everyone knows there will be no real change in the status quo."[41]

Peace plans like these, writes Kathleen Christison, a retired CIA analyst and author of *Perceptions of Palestine,* provide many Israel/Palestine activists with "a comfortable space from which they can promote an amorphous concept of 'peace,' declaring their dedication to 'balance' and giving all-out support by writing letters to politicians and newspapers, without having to face the grim realities of why peace plans are necessary in the first place, or why they always fail," or what, we might add, their ideas would mean in practice for those who would have to live with them, especially Palestinians.

Perhaps the main significance of the Geneva Initiative is that even with all its shortcomings, it appears to be the most conciliatory offer any group of senior Israeli politicians has been able to formulate. Yet while it falls far short of minimum Palestinian demands, not even the Zionist "peace camp," let alone a majority of the electorate, are able to unite around it. Beyond the fact that Israelis have been consistently unwilling to give up most of the settlements as the price for peace, their rejection of the Geneva Initiative is, I believe, a consequence of the peace camp's failure, over so many years, to push for the opportunity to reach for a two-state solution with the Palestinians. The peace camp never had either the strength or the courage to confront Israelis with the choices they faced. Successive Labor governments failed to stop the settlements when they could have done so and failed to tackle the full, complete withdrawal that would likely have satisfied a majority of Palestinians, perhaps opening the door to a solution to the refugee question that took Israeli concerns into account. The leaders of the mainstream Israeli left came to embrace Palestinian statehood warmly in theory while undermining it in practice. The left has repeatedly presented proposals for meaningless and nominal statehood within a greater Israel in which Palestinians get far less than the West Bank and Gaza Strip and Israel keeps its illegal settlements in those areas and overall control. The peace camp, no less than any other political stream in Israel, has failed to treat Palestinians as equals. As a result of its contradictory policies and actions, the peace camp effectively discredited for Israelis the very notion that a negotiated peace was possible, unjustly blaming the Palestinians for the failure of Camp David and ignoring the key roles of repression and settlement expansion in provoking violence. Many ordinary Israelis were thus primed to believe that Palestinians were offered the moon but turned it down in favor of bloodshed. The left paved the way for the new consensus on "unilateral disengagement" forged by Ariel Sharon.

"The state of Israel is coming to an end." For decades, demographer Arnon Soffer has been confronting Israelis with this alarming prophecy. Until a few years ago, Soffer was a prophet in the wilderness, or so he thought, warning his unheeding compatriots that by 2010 the high Palestinian birthrate would result in Arabs outnumbering Jews in historic Palestine—Israel, East Jerusalem, the West Bank, and Gaza Strip. But "suddenly, in the last three years, the scales have fallen from people's eyes," Soffer said in 2004. "The change in public opinion began with the [second] intifada and the Israeli Arab riots, and then the suicide bombings."[42] One Israeli who saw the light was Ariel Sharon. The night Sharon was swept into office in February 2001, Soffer's phone rang. "Bring me your separation maps tomorrow," the voice at the other end demanded. It was Sharon himself. For years, Soffer had worried that Palestinians would realize all they had to do was sit tight until their numbers forced Israeli Jews to give up power. "In order to save the State of Israel," he argued, "we have to separate unilaterally and as quickly as possible." At last, someone was listening, someone with the power to implement Soffer's ideas.

Sharon and his associates' seeming embrace of territorial compromise was far less radical than many have thought. Their views represented a convergence between Israel's mainstream left and right over two central goals: the need to preserve a Jewish majority and maintain control of as many of the settlements as possible. Since the Camp David debacle had discredited the notion of a negotiated partition, the mood was ripe for something else. "The illusion of Oslo has been replaced by a new illusion of unilateral separation," wrote journalist Yacov Ben Efrat. "If Oslo disregarded issues that are central to the Palestinian people, the unilateral agenda disregards the Palestinian people itself."[43]

Ehud Olmert explained that if Israel did nothing as the Palestinian population grew, it would face growing pressure until the only remaining option would be a "a return to the 1967 border, the crushing of Jerusalem, and a struggle to [the] last breath to ward off international pressure to absorb hundreds of thousands of refugees into the shrinking State of Israel." The alternative was "a comprehensive unilateral move," involving minimal withdrawal from settlements, but Israel would "define [its] borders, which under no circumstances will be identical to the Green Line and will include Jerusalem as a united city under [Israeli] sovereignty." The unilateral approach would allow Israel to "define a clear, achievable goal" that would "not depend on the goodwill that its neighbors do not have."[44]

Israel was willing to take a bet that sacrificing a small number of settlements would silence world criticism as it reshaped the country by erecting a "separation wall" across the West Bank, in the process annexing all the major settlements and large tracts of Palestinian land. Palestinians call Gaza the world's largest open-air prison. Yet its status is no different than that of Qalqilya or Bethlehem in the West Bank, surrounded by concrete and cut off from the life around them. According to Dov Weisglass, a senior Sharon adviser who negotiated U.S. backing for the 2005 Gaza disengagement, the plan made "it possible for Israel to park conveniently in an interim situation that distance[d it] as far as possible from political pressure." Under the plan, Israel withdrew approximately eight thousand settlers from the Gaza Strip. But disengagement was no more than "formaldehyde," Weisglass said, to freeze any political process. He claimed that he

> found a device, in cooperation with the management of
> the world [the U.S. administration], to ensure that there

will be no stopwatch here. That there will be no timetable
to implement the settlers' nightmare. I have postponed
that nightmare indefinitely. Because what I effectively
agreed to with the Americans was that part of the settlements would not be dealt with at all, and the rest will not
be dealt with until the Palestinians turn into Finns. That
is the significance of what we did. The significance is the
freezing of the political process. And when you freeze
that process you prevent the establishment of a Palestinian state and you prevent a discussion about the refugees,
the borders and Jerusalem. Effectively, this whole pack-
age that is called the Palestinian state, with all that it
entails, has been removed from our agenda indefinitely.
And all this with authority and permission. All with a
presidential blessing and the ratification of both houses
of Congress. What more could have been anticipated?
What more could have been given to the settlers?[45]

The United States assisted in freezing the process by casting
Sharon's withdrawal of the settlers from Gaza and a few token
settlements in the northern West Bank as a major sacrifice in
the name of peace. Quartet officials from Russia, the European
Union, and the United Nations lavished praise on Israel after
the Gaza pullout.

The reality was that Israel did not end its occupation of the
Gaza Strip. Indeed, according to Israeli officials, Sharon specifically avoided making that claim at the United Nations so as
not to call attention to Israel's continued control.[46] This was
maintained in full over the borders, airspace, and seafront,

along with the establishment of a "Security zone" extending 150 meters into the Gaza Strip.[47] The occupation continued to work by remote control, as was demonstrated during the planning of a Palestinian seaport in Gaza. Haim Ramon, Labor Party minister for economic negotiations with the Palestinians, declared, "We will not let this port be an open port no matter what. We want to control what comes in and what goes out." Ramon told Israel Radio: "If we can't reach an agreement on security arrangements, this port will not be built."[48] Several months after the disengagement, the international envoy to Gaza, former World Bank president James Wolfensohn, complained that Israel is "almost acting as though there has been no withdrawal."[49] By mid-2006, the United Nations Office for the Co-ordination of Humanitarian Affairs reported that the main crossing for goods between Israel and Gaza had been closed by Israel for 60 percent of the time since the start of the year—compared to less than 20 percent of the time in 2004 and 2005, prior to the disengagement. As a direct result, basic foodstuffs like flour, milk, and fruits disappeared from Gaza's markets and hospitals have been forced to ration antibiotics and other essential medications. With more than half of Gaza's population reliant on emergency food aid, U.N. humanitarian officials spoke of widespread hunger.[50]

Olmert's vision of unilateral separation made the point explicitly: "Israel will keep security zones, main settlement blocs, and places important to the Jewish people, first of all, Jerusalem, united under Israeli control."[51] Olmert said that under his party's plan the major settlements of "Ma'ale Adumim, Gush Etzion and Ariel will remain part of the State of

Israel," and that Israel would retain control of the Jordan Valley.[52] The program laid out by Kadima indicated that the "appetite for annexing territory ha[d] not waned for a moment," observed a *Ha'aretz* editorial. The plan merely amounted to more "talk about ending the occupation without ending it."[53]

Olmert called the unilateral solution Israel's "great hope,"[54] but Arnon Soffer, demographic guru, offered a less optimistic prognosis. "Unilateral separation doesn't guarantee 'peace,'" he warned, "it guarantees a Jewish-Zionist state with an overwhelming majority of Jews." What will be the price of this achievement? The "day after unilateral separation," Soffer said, "the Palestinians will bombard us with artillery fire—and we will have to retaliate. But at least war will be at the fence—not in the kindergartens in Tel Aviv and Haifa." Soffer was unambiguous about Israel's response: "We will tell the Palestinians that if a single missile is fired over the fence, we will fire 10 in response. And women and children will be killed and houses will be destroyed." Further down the line, "when 2.5 million people live in a closed-off Gaza," Soffer predicted, "it's going to be a human catastrophe. Those people will become even bigger animals than they are today, with the aid of an insane fundamentalist Islam. The pressure at the border will be awful. It's going to be a terrible war. So, if we want to remain alive, we will have to kill and kill and kill. All day, every day."[55] Indeed, one year after the disengagement, as Palestinians determined to resist learned to circumvent the barriers and build rockets that could reach Israeli towns, Soffer's confidence that Israeli cities would be spared the misery was proven misplaced. Eventually Soffer anticipates that collective imprisonment and the bombardment of the Palestinians will produce "voluntary transfer" through immiseration. "If a Palestinian cannot come into Tel Aviv for work, he will look in Iraq, or Kuwait or London. . . . I believe there will be movement out of the area." The Palestinians will give up their struggle, Soffer believes, and they will "begin to ask for 'conflict management' talks—not that dirty word 'peace.'" And while Israel prospers, separated from the killing fields by walls, it will be the responsibility of the rest of the world to provide "large-scale international aid" to the desperate, dying "animals" living in their Israeli-built cage. Since Israel pulled settlers out of Gaza, the rapidly intensifying violence along the frontier, and the bombardment and return of troops, proved the potency of Soffer's vision. Soffer's comments anticipated almost identical statements made by senior Israeli military officials and ministers in the first weeks after the Gaza pullout.[56] In December 2005, B'Tselem condemned orders reportedly given to soldiers to shoot to kill if anyone entered Israel's self-declared buffer zone in northern Gaza, regardless of the person's identity or reason for being there.[57] Eight months after the withdrawal, the Israeli army reported that it was firing "on average" 300 artillery shells per day at the Gaza Strip,[58] although senior officers conceded that the bombardment, while causing many deaths among Palestinian civilians, was "pointless" and did nothing to prevent fighters firing rockets.[59] Twelve months after the withdrawal, troops returned to the Strip in force, inflicting great privation and carnage on the civilian population, while the bombing of Lebanon that began in July 2006 gave a ghastly illustration of Soffer's vision of killing and killing and killing.

If unilateral separation does not lead to the bloodbath Soffer predicts, at best it would produce what some Israelis, like veteran peace activist Daphna Golan-Agnon, have described as apartheid, with separate roads, separate areas, and separate laws for two populations. "It doesn't matter how we explain it and how many articles are written by Israeli scholars and lawyers," said Golan-Agnon, "there are two groups living in this small piece of land, and one enjoys rights and liberty while the other does not."[60] Unilateral separation offers Israel a Jewish-Zionist state at the price of constant bloodshed and growing Palestinian desperation, which, despite all efforts to wall it out, will deprive Israelis of the normality they crave. It is not a solution, but a dangerous delusion.

CHAPTER THREE

It Could Happen Here

Ever more acutely aware of the "demographic threat," and despairing in the face of escalating violence, a failed peace process, and the false claims of disengagement, many Israelis have turned to a variety of responses, ranging from the absurd to the truly abhorrent. "Am I to understand that you think Israel could commit genocide on the Palestinian people?" was the astonishing question put to prominent Holocaust historian Yehuda Bauer at a seminar sponsored by Yad Vashem's International School for Holocaust Studies in Jerusalem. "Yes," came Bauer's sobering reply. "Just two days ago, extremist settlers passed out flyers to rid Arabs from this land. Ethnic cleansing results in mass killing."[1] But could it really happen? As we have seen, Arnon Soffer has speculated that disengagement could force Palestinians to leave their homeland to escape the resulting economic misery. Is it conceivable that Israel could go further and actually initiate mass expulsions? To what lengths could Israel go to preserve a Jewish majority?

Zionist ideology holds that the Jews of the world need the State of Israel to save them from persecution. Yet Israel's drive to encourage Jewish immigration has more often been motivated by the reality that Jews are needed to save the state. Israeli policymakers, hoping that aggressive efforts to attract immigrants might significantly delay the day when Palestinians once again become the clear majority, have set a goal of one million new immigrants to Israel by 2020.[2]

Mikhail Gorbachev's reforms in the late 1980s paved the way for millions of Jews to leave the Soviet Union and its successor states, and about one million of these emigrants did go to Israel. But it was an uphill struggle to attract them, which suggests that new large-scale immigration is unlikely. Once Gorbachev's liberalization allowed Jews to leave the Soviet Union freely, it quickly became apparent that the majority had no desire to go to Israel; the United States was overwhelmingly their destination of choice. In 1988, Israel's minister of immigration and absorption, Yaakov Zur, decried "the appalling rate of ninety-five percent" of Jews going to destinations other than Israel.[3] Likud activists mounted a campaign calling Jews who went to other countries after being issued Israeli visas "cheats and traitors who exploited us,"[4] and the Israeli government waged an international effort to channel Jews to its shores whether they liked it or not. This included successful pressure to limit the number of Soviet Jews it would accept and efforts to establish direct flights between Moscow and Tel Aviv—finally achieved in 1991—to prevent the "leakage" of Jews from European transit points.[5] Israel's eagerness to keep pace in the demographic race had unintended consequences: The relaxed rules for accepting immigrants from former Soviet countries meant that many who came did not meet the state's strict definition of Jewishness. Hundreds of thousands were Christians and even Muslims from Central Asia, exacerbating the demographic panic and prompting calls in 2002 from Israel's immigration minister, backed by the country's two chief rabbis, to "see to it that families that are completely Christian do not come here—including people who go to church on a regular basis."[6]

Despite the boost from the former Soviet Union, immigration has fallen close to the lowest levels in the state's history.[7] Israel and major American Jewish philanthropists have set up programs, among them Birthright Israel and Masa, which pay for free visits for young North American Jews with the goal of promoting identification with the country and encouraging immigration.[8] The focus on North America is an obvious one. Of the world's estimated 13 million Jews, the largest group—5.7 million—live in the United States. With 5.3 million more in Israel, 95 percent of the remaining 2 million are concentrated in just ten countries.[9] Those with the largest Jewish populations, like the United States, Canada, and France, tend to be stable and prosperous, and the Jewish communities are well-integrated, highly regarded, and essential within their societies. Only the most ideologically motivated minority leave for Israel. No more than 2,000 to 3,000 Jews emigrate annually from North America to Israel and about a quarter of those end up going back home within a few years.[10] In countries from which Jews are still leaving in significant numbers, old trends persist. Two-thirds of the 10,000 Jews who left former Soviet Union countries in 2004 opted to go to Germany instead of Israel, giving Germany the world's fastest-growing Jewish population.[11]

For all Israel invests in attracting immigrants, it is running to stay in place. Net migration per thousand persons has been falling constantly in recent years and reached an estimated zero in 2006.[12] Israel estimates that 760,000 of its citizens—about 12 percent of the total—live permanently abroad, 60 percent of them in North America and 25 percent in Europe.[13] Since former communist states in Eastern Europe joined the European Union, many young Israelis have rushed to apply for EU passports, often from the same countries their parents and grandparents came to Israel to escape.[14] As the opportunities for young Israelis to seek a better life elsewhere increase, it will be ever harder to prevent them from leaving.

In the short term, Israeli leaders and Zionist organizations have realized that only the prospect of severe misfortune could potentially entice Jewish immigration in significant numbers and so they now treat various crises—real, perceived, and exaggerated—around the world as recruitment opportunities. Israeli press and politicians paid close attention to Argentina's economic disaster in 2001–2, always with an eye on how many of the country's 200,000-strong Jewish population might emigrate.[15] Some did answer the call; 6,000 Jewish Argentines moved to Israel in 2002, but the economic crisis eased, and that number fell by nearly 80 percent the following year.[16]

The quest for immigrants has led to inflation of charges that Jews across Europe are facing a new wave of anti-Semitism. Israel's Jewish Agency made plans to send hundreds of emissaries to convince French Jews to emigrate, amid government allegations of French inaction after several anti-Semitic incidents, some of the most heavily publicized of which turned out to be hoaxes or not anti-Semitic attacks at all.[17] Roger Cukierman, the president of CRIF, the umbrella organization of French Jewish organizations, was "shocked and surprised" at the Israeli effort to persuade his countrymen to emigrate and denied that French Jews faced any danger justifying such drastic measures.[18]

Israel's efforts to attract immigrants have at times lurched from the exploitive to the surreal. In 2002, Ashkenazi chief rabbi Israel Meir Lau sent emissaries to seek converts among desperately poor Inca tribespeople in the Andes. The rabbis were under orders to convert only those who were willing to immigrate to Israel on the spot. They found eighteen families, numbering ninety people. The tribespeople, according to one of the missionary rabbis, were "imbued with a love of the Land of Israel that is hard to describe." Airlifted from Peru, the new "Jews" were taken straight from the airport to the West Bank settlements of Alon Shvut and Karmei Tzur, near Bethlehem. One woman, "Batya Mendel," until two months earlier a Peruvian known as Blanca, declared from her new settlement home, "This land was promised eternally by God only to those who were born here. Just because I was born in Peru and don't have Jewish roots makes no difference, because the Book of Zephania states that those who want to believe in the Holy One and be believing Jews—only they have rights to the Land of Israel. Maybe, when the Messiah comes and all the Palestinians are converted to Judaism and believe in God with complete faith, only then will we allow them to live in the Land of Israel." Nachson Ben-Haim, who until he arrived in the settlement was Pedro Mendosa, a taxi driver in the northern Peruvian town of Trujillo, said that he was ready to join the Israeli army "because

I want to defend the country and if there is no choice, I will kill Arabs. But I am sure that Jews kill Arabs only for self-defense and justice, but Arabs do it because they like to kill."[19]

Encouraging Jews to move is one aspect of Israel's immigration policy. The other involves preventing any influx of Arabs. Israel already bars the return of Palestinian refugees, and in 2003, it enacted a law stipulating that a citizen may bring a noncitizen spouse to live in Israel from anywhere in the world, excluding a Palestinian from the occupied territories. The law was aimed at Israel's Arab minority, which, despite enforced separation, maintains strong familial ties to Palestinian communities in the West Bank and Gaza Strip. Under this law, an Israeli citizen choosing to marry a Palestinian from, say, Nablus, in the West Bank would face the choice of either living apart from her spouse or leaving Israel and moving to the West Bank or a third country. Amnesty International, Human Rights Watch, and the International Commission of Jurists denounced the law as racist, as did a handful of Israeli liberals.[20] Hasan Jabarin, the director of Adalah, the Legal Center for Arab Minority Rights in Israel, likened the law to the antimiscegenation measures that existed in the southern United States in the 1950s when mixed-race couples had to leave the state of Virginia to marry legally.[21] Although rare, some Israeli Jews do marry Palestinians from the occupied territories, and they too are victims of this law. Osama Zatar, a Palestinian from the West Bank, met his Israeli-Jewish wife, Jasmin Avissar, at the Jerusalem animal protection organization where they both worked. The couple married in the West Bank, but the law prohibited Osama from living in Israel with

Jasmin. Israeli authorities also refused to allow Jasmin to reside in her husband's hometown of Ramallah, ostensibly because it was under Palestinian Authority control. Jasmin explained their painful dilemma: "We thought of living abroad, but we discovered that no one is willing to give us a visa. . . . And the catch in requesting political asylum is that it will not allow us to come back here should we want to."[22]

As with so many Israeli measures, the initial justification for the law was "security," but when it came up for renewal in 2005, Prime Minister Sharon relieved citizens from pretending that the true intention was not to control demographics. "There's no need to hide behind security arguments," Sharon said, "there is a need for the existence of a Jewish state."[23] The law, renewed with the backing of the Labor Party, will only promote further resentment, conflict, and injustice while doing little to change the demographic reality.

In another desperate move, some have advocated trying to prevent Palestinians from having babies. Israel has already used its social welfare system explicitly to implement selective birth control, according to Yitzhak Kadman, the executive director of Israel's National Council for the Child, who revealed that senior government officials had justified cuts in child allowances that disproportionately affected Orthodox Jews and Arabs, who tend to have more children, on the grounds that they were really designed to reduce the Arab birthrate. The government

even claimed to have statistics, challenged by Kadman, showing that the policy was working.[24]

General Shlomo Gazit, an influential former head of Israeli
military intelligence, told a Jewish Agency–sponsored conference in March 2001 that the "demographic danger is the gravest
one" faced by Israel and necessitated two immediate steps: establishing "a dictatorial regime" for a few years and "restricting the
birthrate in the Arab sector."[25] Dr. Yitzhak Ravid, a senior
researcher at the Israeli government's Armament Development
Authority, called for Israel to "implement a stringent policy of
family planning in relation to its Muslim population." In case his
meaning wasn't clear, Ravid added, "The delivery rooms in
Soroka Hospital in Be'ersheba," an area with a large Bedouin
population, "have turned into a factory for the production of a
backward population."[26] Ravid was speaking in December 2003
at an annual conference of Israel's top military, political, and
business leaders at Herzliya, where his statement generated no
unusual outcry or condemnation. Ravid did not elaborate on
what such a policy might look like, but *Novosti*, a leading
Russian-language newspaper, published an article proposing
that Arab men should be threatened with castration and that
Arab families "who have more than one child" be "deprived of
various benefits, lose their jobs, and [put] under threat of exile."
The article also suggested "cash prizes for young men who vol-
untarily agree to the castration." While it is conceivable that the
article could be the work of a crank, and the paper's editor later
claimed that it had been published in error, *Ha'aretz* columnist
Lily Galili observed, "What is even more surprising than the

fact that the piece got published, is that the paper did not receive any responses from readers or public representatives in the Russian community."[27] In addition to being repulsive, "Imposing measures intended to prevent births within" a specific "national, ethnical, racial or religious group," or incitement to do so, are defined as crimes in the 1951 Convention on the Prevention and Punishment of the Crime of Genocide that was created in the wake of the Nazi holocaust.[28]

While some are considering ways to stop Arabs from having babies, other prominent figures are trying to devise ways to get Israeli Jews to have more children. Following the pattern of affluent Western societies, Israeli Jewish fertility has continually declined. In July 2005, the Jewish People Policy Planning Institute, a think tank established by the Jewish Agency and chaired by Dennis Ross, the former U.S. special Middle East coordinator, issued a report recommending ways to boost Israel's Jewish population, including using tax incentives to encourage childbirth. The report stressed that programs should be designed to encourage families who now have two to three children to have three to four. Israeli Arab families, which tend to be larger in any case, would not gain from the policy, while Jewish families, which usually have fewer children, would see the biggest boost. The report also backed Israeli government policy to "inhibit inflow of non-Jewish immigrants," and proposed a sort of Israeli citizenship–lite aimed mainly at American Jews who have no desire to move to Israel.[29] A U.S.-based group called Russian American Jews for Israel elaborated on what this might look like. In exchange for a one-thousand-dollar "investment" and a week of basic military training in Israel, Jews living abroad would get Israeli passports and would be included in the state's population statistics. The group argued in the proposal it presented to the Israeli government that this might lead to gradual immigration, but more important, it would offer Israel an attractive and quick solution to its "severe demographic and economic difficulties."[30]

The resort to extreme, even repugnant responses has included open discussion of expulsion. For Palestinians, the creation of Israel meant mass, forced dispossession. For many decades, the Israeli establishment rejected any responsibility for this displacement. Beginning in the 1980s, however, a group of Israeli historians who collectively came to be known as "revisionists" or "new historians" confirmed Palestinian accounts primarily using state archives and sources. Palestinian Israeli historian Nur Masalha also demonstrated, with Israeli sources, that within the pre-state Jewish movement in Palestine, the expulsion of Palestinians, or "transfer" as it was commonly called, was seriously debated and contemplated by the Zionist leadership.[31] And into the 1950s, Israeli leaders, with the support of Prime Minister David Ben-Gurion, formulated plans to expel the entire Palestinian Christian population in the Galilee to South America.[32] But by that time, Israel, as a recognized member of the international community, faced constraints that prevented the open pursuit of ethnic cleansing as a policy option. Domestically the idea was widely considered morally unacceptable and unfit for discussion, kept alive almost exclusively by extremists in the Israeli spectrum such as followers of the late Brooklyn-born Rabbi Meir Kahane.

But with the failure of immigration and settlement to decisively shift the demographic balance in favor of Jews, and the collapse of belief in any agreed viable partition, some Israelis are breaking the taboo against advocating expulsion. In 2003, one of the new historians, Benny Morris, published an updated version of his groundbreaking work, *The Birth of the Palestinian Refugee Problem*. Morris concludes that the evidence for the deliberate expulsion of the Palestinian population by the Zionist movement in 1947–49 was even stronger than he had initially thought. On publication, Morris, who had long been viewed as sympathetic to Palestinian claims and a critic of Israel's founders, told *Ha'aretz* journalist Ari Shavit that a "Jewish state would not have come into being without the uprooting of 700,000 Palestinians. Therefore it was necessary to uproot them." He went on, "There are circumstances in history that justify ethnic cleansing." If David Ben-Gurion could be faulted it was because he "did not complete the transfer in 1948."[33] Morris's forthrightness reflected a growing acceptance of such views.

Several political parties—Moledet, Tekuma, and Israel Beitenu—forming the National Union alliance, ran in Israel's 2003 parliamentary election on an explicit platform to expel all Arabs, winning seven seats and a larger share of the vote than Yossi Beilin's Meretz Party. In 2006, running on its own, Israel Beitenu won eleven seats in the 120-seat Knesset, while the other two National Union parties, now joined by the National Religious Party, won nine. Moledet explains on its Web site that it is "an ideological political party in Israel that embraces the idea of population transfer," and it has formulated a "practical plan" to expel Palestinians to Jordan. Moledet boasts that it "has successfully raised the idea of transfer in the public discourse and political arena in both Israel and abroad" while party cadres are "actively involved in establishing these facts on the ground, by encouraging the emigration of displaced and hostile elements from our Land."[34] Moledet was founded by Rehavam Ze'evi, a retired Israeli general, who was assassinated by the Popular Front for the Liberation of Palestine in October 2001 in retaliation for Israel's assassination of that group's leader. "The Arabs of the West Bank have to be transferred to the land of their forefathers," Ze'evi said months before his death, claiming that they had only recently infiltrated into the country. He scorned Israeli liberals who labeled him an extremist, accusing them of hypocrisy: "They forget that Ben-Gurion had a tougher transfer policy than mine."[35]

In September 2004, settlers were among the key founders of a new organization called the National Jewish Front. Cofounder Hen Ben Elyahu explained that its platform "calls for cleansing the region extending from the River Jordan to the Mediterranean from the Goyim [a sometimes derogatory term for non-Jews] and thus guaranteeing a Jewish majority of no less than 90 percent throughout the Land of Israel."[36] And Gamla, an advocacy group founded by former Israeli military officers, Knesset members, and settler activists, published detailed plans for how to carry out the "complete elimination of the Arab demographic threat to Israel" by forcibly expelling all Palestinians and demolishing their towns and villages. This, the plan argued, is "the only possible solution" to the Palestinian-Israeli conflict and is "substantiated by the Torah."[37]

These parties cannot be easily dismissed. They do not, as many would claim, occupy only the fringes of Israeli politics. Rehavam Ze'evi was a cabinet minister at the time of his assassination, and Israel Beitenu's surge in the 2006 election made it a significant player in Israeli coalition politics. The statements by politicians in favor of transfer are widely cited among Palestinians as evidence that Israeli leaders still harbor this intent. Even if most Israeli politicians do not openly advocate expulsion, their tolerance of those who do is alarming. The fact is that none of the National Union or Israel Beitenu leaders have ever been considered beyond the pale by Israel's mainstream parties. Between 2001 and late 2004, all the National Union party leaders served as cabinet ministers, at times in coalitions with the Labor Party. "An evil spirit is infiltrating public discourse: the spirit of expulsion," warned Israeli historian Tom Segev. "The danger lies when the possibility of transfer becomes part of the political discourse, when it seemingly becomes a legitimate subject."[38]

Israel's outspoken Jewish allies in the United States have failed to condemn—or, by their own admission, even notice—this advocacy of ethnic cleansing. When asked about the inclusion of the National Union parties in the Israeli government after the 2003 election, AIPAC press secretary Rebecca Needler replied that "Israel's coalition government is representative of a true democracy." Abraham Foxman, national director of the Anti-Defamation League, which boasts of "90 years fighting anti-Semitism, bigotry and extremism," considered it "an overstatement to say that the [National Union parties] ran on a platform of transfer," attributing the position to the personal views of a few individual members.[39] However, Moledet's Web site, in English and Hebrew, is quite explicit. At this, Foxman changed tack, arguing that since "transfer" was not part of the Israeli government's coalition agreement there was no reason for the ADL to issue a public comment, although he himself thought the idea of transfer was "unacceptable" and "undemocratic."[40]

Perhaps in part because of the silence of figures like Foxman, advocates of ethnic cleansing have made some inroads in the United States.[41] Benny Elon, Ze'evi's successor as leader of Moledet, has focused on building long-term support for expulsion among devout Christians in the United States. "For the enterprise to survive," Elon explains, "we need to gain legitimacy in the minds of the people here in Israel and in America." This means playing on Christian fundamentalist beliefs so that a large segment of the American public comes to see the Israeli-Palestinian conflict not as a political or foreign policy question, but as a matter of religious faith, like opposition to abortion or the teaching of evolution. Moledet has warm ties with the Christian right and evangelical leaders including Pat Robertson and Gary Bauer. "In America the Christians are willing to listen," explains Elon, and when he goes to meet with senior congressional leaders, "I am coming at the request of their constituents and supporters."[42] Elon's message has found public support among some U.S. lawmakers. Oklahoma senator James Inhofe told the Senate in 2002 that Israel should not be required to return any of the territories it captured in 1967, "because God said so." Inhofe asserted, "This is not a political battle at all," but "a contest over whether or not the word of God is true."[43] At the height of Israel's assault on Jenin refugee camp in early May 2002, then House majority leader Dick Armey, a Texas Republican, argued forcefully on national television that he was "content to have Israel grab the entire West Bank" and that the Palestinians should be expelled.[44] Elon has studied the strategy of the Israeli Peace Camp in its heyday. He points to Oslo: There is "something that Yossi Beilin and his crew of suits understood. . . . Rabin got stuck on the eleventh round of negotiations on the Madrid plan in Washington. Beilin was waiting in the wings." Elon sees his movement playing a similar role: "When the Road Map explodes we'll be waiting with our alternative plan, ready to execute it on a moment's notice. That is what I am working towards."[45]

How real is the danger that Elon's dream could become the Middle East's new nightmare? The displacement of some half a million Lebanese citizens during the Israeli bombing in July 2006 demonstrates the frightening ease with which "transfer" could be carried out from the point of view of Israeli Jews. In March 2002, 46 percent favored "transferring" Palestinians from the occupied territories and 60 percent favored "encouraging" Palestinian citizens of Israel to leave Israel, according to a poll by Tel Aviv University's Jaffee Center for Strategic Studies.[46] Three years later, a poll by Israel's Dahaf Institute found that among Jewish Israelis 59 percent agreed that "the state should encourage Israeli Arabs to emigrate."[47] While the March 2002 poll possibly reflects the immediate response to bloody events (multiple suicide bombings occurred in Israel during that month), the consistent support for such ideas is deeply troubling. The polls reflect the failure of Israeli and Zionist leaders to condemn and marginalize the purveyors of such poison.

Yet we can also read the polls in a different way. While some Israeli Jews certainly harbor implacable hatred for Palestinians, many, like those Palestinians who say they support attacks on civilians, are reacting out of anger, trauma, and frustration at a hardening stalemate. More Israelis will surely fall into the waiting arms of Elon and company after disengagement fails to deliver the promised respite, if we are unable to develop an alternative vision. Israelis and Palestinians desire hope. As we have seen, all efforts to realize peace through partition have failed. With the Israeli-Palestinian deadlock only deepening, how can we justify refusing to explore other ideas? Let us now turn to a different vision, one of peace based on reconciliation and universal human rights.

CHAPTER FOUR

A United, Democratic State in Palestine-Israel

"No eye can see, no ear can hear, no mind can comprehend what heaven is like." Rabbi Yohanan Ben Zakkai, writing in the first century, has gone some way to explain why the human imagination is more readily able to depict the torments of hell than the ecstasy of the hereafter. Describing a joint Israeli-Palestinian state and what it might look like is scarcely any easier. There is no shortage of arguments as to why such a state is impossible. But for now, let us put them aside. Instead, let's take a fresh look at the situation in Palestine-Israel. Two peoples are locked in a struggle over legitimate control of the country and everything implied in that control. On both sides the ideals are so strongly held that rather than change them to fit the reality of the situation, both peoples propose solutions to change the reality. This is essentially what all the two-state plans have attempted to do: Shift some settlers here, force Palestinians over there, bridge this unbridgeable wedge of land, keep refugees far away, and hope that with enough walls and security forces an edifice built on injustice, expulsion, inadequate resources, and discrimination can be kept from collapse. What if we took a different approach? What if we accept that, today, Israelis and Palestinians inhabit the same country and that any attempt to separate them has only exacerbated the conflict because partition requires each side to give up more than it is able. What if we tried to join them together instead in a single democratic state?

Creating a single state with equal rights for Israeli Jews and Palestinians could in theory resolve the most intractable issues: the fate of Israeli settlements built since 1967, the rights of Palestinian refugees, and the status of Jerusalem. What if an Israeli Jew who wanted to live in Hebron, or a Palestinian who chose to move to Tel Aviv or Jaffa, was simply able to do so? For Israeli Jews, the key goals of Zionism would be realized: If not a monopoly on power, they would have a permanent, protected, and vibrant national presence in all of Israel-Palestine, as partners and equals, not as occupiers. Palestinians, for their part, would gain the rights they are currently denied. The obstacles are formidable, particularly those related to private property and compensation. But precedents do exist, and I believe these issues would be much easier to deal with in the context of national reconciliation.

The idea of a single state in Palestine-Israel is not a new one and has its antecedents among both Palestinians and Zionists. In the pre-state Zionist movement a small but prominent group of intellectuals, including the founding president of the Hebrew University, Judah Magnes, and philosophers Martin Buber and

Hannah Arendt argued staunchly against partition. Magnes predicted that partition would be impractical and bound to lead to further conflict because it could ultimately satisfy neither community. Buber, who moved to Palestine from Nazi Germany in 1938, warned that the Zionist program "to create a Jewish majority" was fatally flawed and would mean "war—real war—with our neighbors, and also with the whole Arab nation: for what nation will allow itself to be demoted from the position of majority to that of a minority without a fight?"[1]

In 1947, the Ihud (Union) association, uniting many of these thinkers, published a book arguing for "an undivided binational Palestine composed of two equal nationalities, Jews and Arabs." The state would have equal representation of Jews and Arabs throughout the government.[2] Buber supported a single state conjoining the Arab and Jewish communities that would be imbued with "complete equality of rights between the two partners, disregarding the changing numerical relationship between them; and with joint sovereignty founded upon these principles—such an entity would provide both peoples with all that they truly need. If such a state were established, neither people would have to fear any longer domination of the other through numerical superiority."[3] With hindsight, the warnings from those like Buber and Magnes appear prophetic, but at the time their proposed solutions stood no chance of wider support. Most Zionists insisted on Jewish sovereignty and were simply not interested in the kind of partnership they were discussing. Palestinians, for their part, saw Buber and others as being part of the Zionist movement that was colonizing Palestine and saw no reason why they should share equal power with recent arrivals who were still a minority and whose intention they feared was to take over the entire country. When in 1925 Buber had, along with a number of other prominent Zionist and Jewish intellectuals in the peace group Brith Shalom (Covenant of Peace), called for "mutual social relations on the basis of absolute political equality of two culturally autonomous peoples,"[4] the Jewish population in Palestine was just over 80,000—a mere tenth of the total population.

The call for a single state reemerged years later from within the Palestinian national movement in the 1960s when Palestinians had begun to regroup after the traumatic dispersal of 1948 and organize under their own leadership. They had started to grapple with the reality that any liberation strategy required them to have some position on the fate of Israelis, or "Jewish settlers," as they were often called. In 1969, Golda Meir infamously stated that "[t]here were no such thing as Palestinians" and asserted, "It was not as though there was a Palestinian people in Palestine considering itself as a Palestinian people and we came and threw them out and took their country away from them. They did not exist."[5] Such widely held views constituted a major obstacle for Palestinians, even those who could foresee reconciliation. Recognition had to be reciprocal and the notion of recognizing Israel's "right to exist," while Israeli leaders denied the existence of Palestinians, was simply unthinkable. But within the PLO there was a serious and wide-ranging debate about how to conceive of a future relationship with the Jews in Palestine, and positions, both official and unofficial, evolved markedly from total rejection to acceptance. The stance eventually adopted by the PLO, which involved compromises between many different factions, did not reflect the depth of thinking that went on. For example, a leader of the PLO's dominant Fatah faction argued in 1969 that:

> [t]here is a large Jewish population in Palestine and it has grown considerably in the last twenty years. We recognize that it has the right to live there and that it is part of the Palestinian people. We reject the formula that the Jews must be driven into the sea. If we are fighting a Jewish state of a racial kind, which had driven the Arabs out of their lands, it is not so as to replace it with an Arab state which would in turn drive out the Jews. What we want to create in the historical borders of Palestine is a multiracial democratic state . . . a state without any hegemony, in which everyone, Jew, Christian or Muslim will enjoy full civic rights.[6]

The PLO did ultimately adopt the goal of a secular, democratic state in all Palestine as its official stance. Yet the dominant view in the Palestinian resistance movement in the 1960s was that armed struggle was the only way to liberate Palestine, and that there could be no negotiation or compromise with the "Zionist leaders."[7] This was in line with other anticolonial and revolutionary movements of the period but it meant there was no strategy to appeal directly to, or build alliances with, segments of the Israeli population. The constraints, compromises, and revolutionary rhetoric of the time meant that the PLO never developed a clear and persuasive vision for a democratic state that could present a credible challenge to Zionism's insistence on the necessity of a Jewish monopoly. Eventually, under international pressure, the PLO abandoned its earlier positions, sought negotiations with Israel, and accepted the notion of partition, which thus far has meant at best Palestinian autonomy under overall Israeli control. But if a single state was unthinkable in the past, many of the conditions that made it so have changed. Perhaps the most important is that the majority of Israelis and Palestinians now understand that the other community is here to stay.

The main attraction of a single-state democracy is that it allows all the people to live in and enjoy the entire country while preserving their distinctive communities and addressing their particular needs. It offers the potential to deterritorialize the conflict and neutralize demography and ethnicity as a source of political power and legitimacy. There are many ways to imagine how such a state might be constituted. It could, for instance, be a federation or a unitary state; it could adopt a parliamentary or presidential system. I do not intend to lay out here a detailed constitution, but simply to give some preliminary consideration to what an Israel-Palestine state might look like, in the hope that this will invite broader discussion. But for this single state to prosper, it would have to rest on common values and its chosen structure be able to fulfill a clear set of functions and goals. What follows are eight principles for the one-state solution, rooted in the Universal Declaration of Human Rights and informed by such worthy models as the Belfast Agreement signed by parties to the conflict in Northern Ireland:

1. The power of the government shall be exercised with rigorous impartiality on behalf of all the people in the diversity of their identities and traditions and shall be founded on the principles of full respect for and equality of civil, political, social, and cultural rights, and of freedom from discrimination for all citizens, women and men, and of parity of esteem and of just and equal treatment for the identity, ethos, and aspirations of all communities.

2. The constitution recognizes that the state is formed by the free and consenting union of two principal national communities, Israeli Jews and Palestinians, which each have multiple subcultures, shared histories, and sometimes irreconcilable narratives binding them to the country. Citizens of the state can call it a Jewish state or a Palestinian state if they wish to identify it as such. It will be both equally, simultaneously, and without contradiction. It is possible to be a full citizen of the state without belonging to either of these communities.

3. The state, recognizing the distinctive identities of the national communities who live in it, supports their linguistic and cultural traditions and production, all of which are part of the cultural wealth of the country. The state has mechanisms for national communities to exercise autonomy in decision-making related to language, education,

culture, and other matters, but which do not foster inter-ethnic competition, discrimination, or separatism.

4. The state guarantees the freedom of religion and worship of every citizen and does not interfere in the affairs of religious communities. The state is neutral among religious groups and any state funding for religious schools or other institutions is distributed in a nondiscriminatory, transparent, and equitable manner.

5. While it is recognized that victims have a right to remember their history and to contribute to a changed society, the state enables all its citizens to participate in developing shared public spaces and symbols, as well as celebrations of common citizenship and identity that can be inclusive of people from every community.

6. The state recognizes that Israeli Jews have a special relationship with Jewish communities outside the country, and that Palestinians and Israeli Jews of Arab origin are connected to the broader Arab world and to Arab diasporic communities, and that all are free to maintain and develop these vital relationships.

7. The state, recognizing that Israel-Palestine is a focus for adherents of the three monotheistic faiths all over the world, accepts that it has a special responsibility to ensure protection and access to all holy places.

8. The state actively fosters economic opportunity, social justice, and a dignified life for all its citizens, and establishes fair and efficient mechanisms to compensate victims of the conflict and redress inequalities caused by unjust practices in the past.

These principles attempt to balance the need and desire for cultural autonomy and self-determination that many Israeli Jews and Palestinians feel with the need for a government that does not encourage ethnic or territorial competition, promotes interaction among all its citizens, and protects the rights of everyone, including those who choose not to identify with a particular national group. We now have to imagine structures that can give effect to these principles, and here it is particularly useful to look at some of the solutions developed by democratic countries that have successfully managed long-standing conflicts over rights and power between ethnic, religious, and linguistic communities, such as Canada, Belgium, South Africa, and India.[8]

Belgium today is generally dismissed as a boring country where little happens. Palestine-Israel should be so lucky. In fact, Belgium offers some important lessons. Its modern history has been bedeviled by bitter conflict and rivalry between its main communities, Flemish people in the north of the country, who speak Dutch, and Walloons in the south, who speak French. The conflict originated after Belgium gained independence in 1830. During the state's first century, French speakers held a monopoly on political power, excluding the vast majority of Dutch speakers from participation in government and administration. As Flemings became an absolute majority of the population, and their traditional involvement in trade rather than manufacturing increasingly drove the national economy, they began to assert demands for full rights and recognition. A conflict that began over language gradually developed ethnic-cultural dimensions and hardened into a seemingly irreconcilable confrontation. As

Flemish nationalism grew, it was mirrored by Walloons, who feared that their economic and demographic decline made them vulnerable to Flemish domination.

The acrimony between the two communities dominated Belgian politics throughout the twentieth century, and the country often experienced unstable government and on rare occasions violence, amid threats from politicians in one or the other community to seek secession. This move could quickly turn an effort to divide the country into a civil war. To defuse the conflict and keep the country together, Belgium has in recent decades undertaken a gradual process of constitutional reform, transforming the state from a unitary to a federal form. There is a national federal government with responsibility for the economy, social security, foreign affairs, and other matters. In addition, the country is divided into three self-governing regions, the Flemish region, which is officially Dutch speaking, the Walloon region, which is officially French speaking, and the Brussels-Capital region, composed of nineteen officially bilingual communes. This transformation is instructive for Israelis and Palestinians.

In a democracy, a national government is expected to represent and serve all its citizens impartially. The earliest elections held under a simple one-person, one-vote majoritarian system might produce a well-balanced parliament in terms of Israeli Jewish and Palestinian members, but in the long run, as the population shifts, more Arabs would likely be elected. Given the history of antagonism, Israeli Jews may well fear discrimination as the new minority population. Separate Jewish and Arab voter rolls or candidate lists would be one way to solve the problem.

But in addition to being complex, such measures would run fundamentally counter to the notion of "one person, one vote."

Ultimately it is to be hoped that the Palestinian-Jewish divide does not remain the principal fault line in the political system. It seems likely that left to their own devices most Palestinians would vote for Arab-dominated parties and most Jews would vote for Jewish-dominated parties. But there are good reasons to believe that over time such distinctions can diminish and broad cross-national coalitions could form over economic, environmental, educational, and other concerns. Both Israeli Jewish and Palestinian societies are highly diverse, which makes it difficult to predict the sorts of alliances that would emerge. Within Israel a significant number of Arab voters have traditionally supported the Labor Party for economic and social policy reasons despite its alienating Zionist ideology. Palestinian citizens of Israel make up 22 percent of Labor Party members and form the largest single constituency among the party's various blocs, their numbers increasing from 14,600 members in 2002 to 21,500 in 2005.[9] There is also a strong tradition of joint Arab-Jewish parties on the far left that can set an example. One can imagine that Palestinian and Israeli business interests might well come together to form rightist groupings, while parties representing economically and socially excluded Israeli Jews and Palestinians would find common ground (the socioeconomic disparities among Jewish communities in Israel are formidable). It is also not impossible to imagine conservative Muslim and Jewish parties forming alliances to lobby for common concerns. This is the future; in the beginning it might be necessary to design a system that promotes balanced representation without compromising the principle that citizens are not distinguished by ethnicity when it comes to electing a national government. In this, Belgium sets an important and cautionary example.

About 60 percent of Belgium's population lives in the Flemish region, while the once politically dominant Walloons comprise about a third. At the federal level, Belgium has a parliamentary system with universal suffrage. There are eleven multimember geographic electoral districts to which seats are allocated based on population. This means that the Flemish region elects about 60 percent of the seats in parliament (88 out of 150 at the 2003 general election). It has long been a convention, however, that the federal government should have an equal number of Dutch-speaking and French-speaking ministers who take decisions by consensus, and it became a constitutional requirement in the early 1990s. Other "alarm bell" procedures in the Belgian constitution include a mechanism to hold up decisions opposed by three-quarters of the people in either community. The Palestinian Authority elections included a quota ensuring that Christians were voted into at least a certain proportion of seats, so the principle of implementing special protections to ensure adequate representation has found some acceptance among Palestinians.

Belgian political parties are unilingual and run candidates only in their own regions, a peculiarity that stems from the near linguistic homogeneity of the populations in each area. Israeli Jews and Palestinians may actually be better positioned to develop truly cross-community politics. The Belgian model shows that it is possible to build modest safeguards that are compatible with a modern one-person, one-vote democracy.

There are any number of ways to devise such a system, the key goal being to provide the minimal necessary reassurance that state power will not be abused by one community to dominate another. These arrangements could be transitional, long-term, or, as in Belgium, permanent.

Overall, Belgium's continuous process of constitutional reform has led to the decline of separatist sentiment in both the Flemish and Walloon regions.[10] But the country's ethno-linguistic divisions have by no means disappeared and have to be actively managed all the time. The words of a professor at Louvain University railing against Walloon nationalists who refuse to utter a word of Dutch seemed terribly familiar, as did his condemnation of Flemings in Brussels who "dream of 'flemishiz-ing' the city once and for all, by buying it up piece by piece and building a wall that is symbolic if not physical" between its communities.[11] Such hostilities cannot be eliminated by the stroke of a pen, but a constitution can provide a framework to navigate them, first to stop them from becoming deadly, and second to create possibilities that might allow them to heal with time.

Beyond a national government that brings Israeli Jews and Palestinians together, how could the two communities exercise substantial autonomy over their own affairs? An obvious possibility is that the country be divided into self-governing regions, perhaps one Jewish and one Arab, with Jerusalem, like Brussels, being administered as a binational region and capital. Canada, like Belgium, has used federalism to manage the conflict between French-speaking Quebec and English Canada, whose history of political domination and discrimination against Quebeckers generated fierce resistance. This idea is not new. In 1947, the UN voted to partition Palestine into separate Arab and Jewish states. However, a minority proposal from India, Yugoslavia, and Iran suggested creating a federal state with autonomous Arab and Jewish regions. However, while the main communities in Belgium and Canada have fought over political power and rights, there are no significant territorial disputes involved; the boundaries of the Flemish and Walloon regions, for example, are not seriously contested as long as there is no threat of outright secession by any community. For this reason, it is possible to maintain a federation between well-defined and largely homogenous territorial entities.[12] The attempt to create a federation in Palestine-Israel, where agreement on any kind of territorial partition has been impossible and the populations are at once segregated but territorially intertwined, might invite the communities back to feuding over land. The advantages of federation that allow maximum autonomy may be outweighed by the dangers of ongoing territorial conflict and demographic manipulation. Addressing these concerns, Meron Benvenisti, Israeli geographer and former deputy mayor of Jerusalem, has argued that a "bizonal" federated republic with no fences or walls between its constituent Palestinian and Israeli regions is a model worthy of study.[13]

Another structure used in Belgium may provide a way to benefit from the advantages of federalism while minimizing the risk of renewed territorial strife. In addition to federal and regional layers of government with jurisdictions over specific territories, Belgium has a parallel system of "community government." The constitution recognizes that the country is made up of three communities: Dutch speakers, French speakers, and German speakers. Each group is entitled to elect a community government with its own parliament and executive that has responsibility in education, culture, language, and even international relations in some spheres.[14] An Israeli Jewish community government along these lines, for example, could be responsible for Jewish education, Hebrew language media, support for Hebrew and Jewish arts, and relations with Jewish communities outside the country. A system combining nonterritorial community governments, alongside a national government representing all citizens, if carefully crafted, could provide the basis for a stable, peaceful, and prosperous country.

While the structure of government might draw on a number of useful models, many of the key challenges to an Israeli-Palestinian state are unique and specific. Palestinian refugee rights are one such challenge and they have proved an insurmountable obstacle to a two-state solution. Most Palestinians refuse to contemplate abandoning the right of those who were expelled or fled from their homes in 1947–49 or subsequently to return and receive compensation if they choose. Israeli Jews have adamantly and almost unanimously rejected this right because of the obvious demographic implications for the continued existence of a Jewish state. The Law of Return, which is an Israeli policy not grounded in any international law, allows anyone the state recognizes as a Jew to gain citizenship in the country. This law is viewed as racist by Palestinians because while a Jew, born, say, in Argentina, can "return" to a country she has never visited, a Palestinian refugee born in Jaffa and all her descendants are condemned to permanent exile. Although the dangers faced by Jews around the world have clearly diminished, the Law of Return should nonetheless be preserved in order to recognize the special connection Jewish communities have with Israeli Jews. This relationship has been complex and contentious, but its resolution should be left to those involved in it. If any Jew wishes to immigrate to the country and help build it, she should be welcomed.

As for the rights of Palestinian refugees, implementing them is a necessary part of justice and reconciliation. The right of return belongs to Palestinian refugees as individuals and it is not for other Palestinians or Israelis to seek to abolish it.[15] As of March 2005, there were 4.2 million Palestinian refugees registered to receive services from UNRWA, the United Nations Relief and Works Agency for Palestine Refugees in the Near East, which has provided basic health, education, and employment to Palestinian refugees for nearly sixty years. Nearly 700,000 of these refugees live in the West Bank, and some 1 million in the Gaza Strip (almost 80 percent of Gaza's population). The remaining 2.6 million UNRWA-registered refugees live in Jordan, Lebanon, and Syria. Estimates vary for the number of Palestinians who are either unregistered refugees or who live as exiles, immigrants, and citizens in other countries.

It is impossible to predict how many Palestinians would want to return, but it is unlikely to be all of them. For many, return will not be a single act but a process and a relationship. Palestinians who are well established in Jordan, the United States, or Canada might want to make annual visits home, or perhaps retire in their family's ancestral village or in a condominium on the seafront. Certainly many refugees, particularly those in refugee camps in Lebanon, will want to return permanently. This is a right recognized in international law and it is difficult to imagine an end to the conflict without the refugees being able to exercise it.

Israel has gained practical experience absorbing large numbers of immigrants, experience that will be needed to make that return successful. It cannot be haphazard but must be organized and planned using all the available resources and knowledge along with significant international aid. According to Palestinian geographer Salman Abu-Sitta, the author of extensive analyses of the country's geography and demography, the areas from which the majority of Palestinian refugees originated are inhabited by "only 1.5 percent of the Israeli population," while "90 percent of [former Palestinian] village sites are still vacant today."[16] Abu-Sitta has argued on this basis that return is feasible for most rural Palestinians and can be carried out without displacing Israelis.[17] With respect to the major cities, Abu-Sitta has argued that there is sufficient space for those Palestinians wishing to return to build new homes on "city land without necessarily evicting the present Jewish occupants as done by Israel to the Palestinians in 1948," allowing "returnees to live in harmony with the present Jewish inhabitants."[18] For decades Israel has neglected to develop the largely Arab-populated but sparse Galilee and Negev areas, having concentrated so much of its resources on military spending and settling the West Bank. These regions could be developed with new towns both for returning refugees and for other citizens of the country.

Every year for over five decades, the United Nations has reaffirmed Resolution 194, which demands that "refugees wishing to return to their homes and live in peace with their neighbors should be permitted to do so at the earliest practicable date, and that compensation should be paid for the property of those choosing not to return and for loss or damage to property. . . ." It is clear that under international law, the right of return comes with an obligation that all returning refugees be ready to live in peace. This aspect is just as important as return itself. Preserving the Law of Return, as a gesture to the Jewish citizens of the country, and respecting the right of return will be a symbolic and practical affirmation that the new state is simultaneously the Jewish state and the Palestinian state, and that it fulfills the aspirations of both peoples and recognizes their equality.

One of the toughest problems any peace settlement will have to address is the competing claims over property. This would likely be at the top of the agenda of any transitional regime. In the Palestinian exodus of 1947–49 hundreds of thousands of people lost all their property, including farms, orchards, stores, and fully furnished houses. Entire villages were emptied. Many of these villages were later destroyed by Israel both to prevent return of the residents and to erase the fact of their existence. In the major cities like Jerusalem, Haifa, and Acre, much of the property was seized under the Absentee Property Law (1950) and handed over to the Jewish National Fund, which allocates it exclusively to Jews. As Jewish immigrants and refugees flooded into Israel in its first years, the government settled people in these homes. After 1967, a similar process began in East Jerusalem and the rest of the occupied territories, as Israel began to seize Palestinian-owned land for settlement building and more recently for construction of the separation wall and the exclusion zone around it. The issue of property is closely tied to the question of the rights of refugees, and no doubt many Israelis currently oppose the return of Palestinians not only because of the fear for their safety and of the effect on the country's demographics, but because they might lay claim to homes and lands that have been inhabited by Israeli Jews for decades. The problem is difficult but not insoluble, and any political settlement that tries to avoid this issue can only store up more bitterness in the long run.

A just and stable solution must by definition settle property claims fairly and transparently through compensation and, where achievable within the context of reconciliation, restitution. It is impossible to simply rewind the clock of history, and as hard as it is, a great many Palestinians will have to face the reality that the properties they left behind no longer exist, in which case they will have to accept compensation. In other cases, it may not be in the public interest to allow return to original properties. Such painful decisions can only be made by a democratic government operating according to principles of strict nondiscrimination and seeking the good of the entire population, not just part of it. Impartial bodies could be set up to adjudicate claims, and a commitment made by all that no one will be left destitute by the process. Once there is a commitment to equality and a system for enforcing rights, it is possible to devise many solutions that do justice without creating new victims. The challenge will be to allow individuals to seek redress, while giving social reconciliation the best chance of succeeding.

In the 1950s, hundreds of thousands of Arab Jews who immigrated to Israel were deprived of their property in Arab countries, particularly Iraq and Egypt. Some pro-Israel organizations have tried to use this fact to claim that an "exchange of populations" took place that in effect invalidates the Palestinian right to return or to reclaim property. This argument makes a mockery of the principles of refugee and property rights, because it conceives of people not as individual human beings with inherent right, but treats them according to a nineteenth-century perspective in which individuals are merely members of ethnonational groups who can be pushed across borders to suit the political interests of states. The argument is also somewhat disingenuous because the emigration, sometimes in an atmosphere of coercion of Jews from Arab countries, which occurred after the 1947–49 exodus of Palestinians, was welcomed by the Zionist movement, which would not have been content had Israel's own population remained small while large numbers of Jews lived elsewhere in the Arab world. The correct response to the tragedy of Arab Jews being forced from their homes is to support their right to return, restitution, and compensation on exactly the same basis as we should support those rights for Palestinians. Advocating for the rights of its

Israeli Jewish citizens who have been unjustly deprived of property in the Arab world or anywhere else should be part of the policy of a joint Israeli-Palestinian state.

The settlements Israel has built in the occupied territories since 1967 are related to property claims. A major obstacle to the establishment of a Palestinian state, most settlements could simply remain where they are in a unified country. Palestinians whose land was confiscated for the use of settlements would need to receive full compensation, and the relationship of the settlements to other communities would have to change completely. They would become ordinary towns, and Palestinian towns and cities and other Israeli towns long deprived of resources would have to gain access to the kinds of funding for development and infrastructure that were long reserved for the settlements. The state would have to introduce modern laws ensuring nondiscrimination in housing to end the decades-old Israeli system of establishing what are in effect Jewish-only areas. It is likely that the majority of Israeli Jews and Palestinians would continue to live close to those with whom they identify, but there can be no legal impediment to people living where they want to.

The fundamental pillar of a peaceful, democratic Israeli-Palestinian society is an effective educational system: In every society the education system is used to try to instill in children the values and identity of their community. But here we would start from a very difficult and unequal situation. Currently, within Israel's 1948 borders, Jewish and Arab children attend separate and unequal schools. Palestinian citizens of Israel have long complained that the curriculum their children must study emphasizes Zionist values to which they can never aspire because those values only include Jews. They also feel that the curriculum distorts and downplays Arab and Palestinian history.[19] But it is in the disparities in funding where Israeli discrimination is most starkly visible. A Human Rights Watch study found that the consistently inferior funding and support received by Arab schools meant that, "by virtually every measure, Palestinian Arab children receive an inferior education to their counterparts in the Jewish public education system."[20] Another study found that excluding teacher salaries, schools in central and northern Israel had on average $1,097 to spend for each Jewish child, while Arab schools had just $191 for each of their students. In the south of the country, there was just $60 spent per Arab child, while the state spent $1,535 per capita on the children of Jewish settlers in the West bank.[21]

Palestinian children in the occupied West Bank and Gaza Strip attend schools operated either by UNRWA or the Palestinian Authority. Conditions for these children are considerably worse even than those for Palestinian citizens of Israel. Due to the desperate lack of resources, average class sizes range from forty to fifty pupils per teacher, and in the West Bank and Gaza Strip, most schools operate double shifts. The challenge to reverse this legacy is compounded by the damaging effects of the occupation. Indeed UNRWA underlines that its work in the occupied territories is carried out under particularly difficult conditions because

[c]hildren's learning and the education system as a whole have been severely disrupted by armed conflict, closures, curfews and access problems since the start of the inti- fada. A total of 121 pupils have been killed and 1,532 injured as a result of direct military action. In some instances, pupils have been killed or injured while in class. Hundreds of thousands of teaching days have been lost.[22]

At the same time, the Israeli government and U.S.-based pro- Israel groups have consistently claimed that Palestinian schools, particularly the textbooks they use, teach anti-Israeli and anti- Semitic "incitement" on a wide scale. U.S. politicians seeking to curry favor with pro-Israel constituencies have picked up this mantra. New York senator Hillary Clinton, for example, boasted in her address to the 2005 convention of AIPAC, "I stood with my friend, Elie Wiesel, to denounce this incitement, this vio- lence, this anti-Semitism in Palestinian textbooks" and scolded, "How do we expect to have a democratically elected Palestinian government if their textbooks are still preaching such hatred, and if we allow this dehumanizing rhetoric to go unchallenged?"

What are the facts? Until the past few years, Palestinian stu- dents in the West Bank used the Jordanian government curricu- lum, because this was the status quo at the time of the occupation, while in Gaza, Egyptian textbooks were used. Since the mid-1990s, the Palestinian Authority has been creating its own textbooks, and probably no school curriculum develop- ment project has been as closely monitored by outsiders. The fact is that every serious study of Palestinian textbooks has found the claims of "incitement" to be utterly baseless. An independent study of Palestinian textbooks by Professor Nathan Brown of George Washington University in 2001 noted that "virtually every discussion in English on Palestinian education repeats the charge that Palestinian textbooks incite students against Jews and Israel." Brown states that "[i]t may therefore come as a surprise to readers that the books authored under the PNA [Palestinian National Authority] are largely innocent of these charges. What is more remarkable than any statements they make on the subject is their silence—the PNA-authored books often stubbornly avoid treating anything controversial regarding Palestinian national identity, forcing them into awkward omissions and gaps."[23]

A series of studies conducted by the Israel/Palestine Center for Research and Information (IPCRI) came to a similar conclusion and found that the new books promote tolerance, peace and conflict resolution, critical thought, and open-mindedness.[24] "A Study of the Impact of the Palestinian Curriculum," commissioned by the Belgian Technical Cooperation at the end of 2004, and conducted by education experts Dr. Roger Avenstrup and Dr. Patti Swarts, confirmed that these peace-oriented values were present throughout the Palestinian curriculum, but the authors concluded that

[i]n the light of the debate stirred by accusations of incitement to hatred and other criticisms of the Palestinian textbooks, there is no evidence at all of that happening as a result of the curriculum. What is of great concern to students, teachers and parents alike is that although they wish it, students find it difficult to accept peace and conflict

resolution as a solution to the conflict, and teachers find it difficult to teach, while soldiers and settlers are shooting in the streets and in schools, and checkpoints have to be braved every day. It would seem that the occupation is the biggest constraint to the realization of these values in the Palestinian curriculum.[25]

The growing anger and resistance generated by the occupation as well as a history of inadequate schools will stand as extraordinary obstacles to effective education. The picture is not entirely bleak, however: Both Israeli and Palestinian societies have historically placed enormous emphasis on education. Israel has done this by handsomely funding Israeli Jewish schools and developing world-class universities, while Palestinians traditionally have had to rely on themselves, with families often investing all their savings to send their children to universities overseas. For Palestinians, as it was for generations of persecuted Jews in Europe, the quest for education has been a means to escape the limits imposed by an unjust world.

What would education look like in a new democratic state? Clearly, an immediate correction in the enormous disparities in resources is required. All children must be entitled to the same standards of education. In the short run, each Israeli school could, where practical, be twinned with a nearby Palestinian school to share some facilities, and to provide early, positive contact among children who would together learn the values of a joint society. Immediate steps would need to be taken to reform curricula that denigrate any community, including Israeli Jewish texts that distort or exlude Palestinian history. In the long term, the society would have to decide whether Israeli Jews and Palestinians would attend separate schools defined by languages, as in Belgium and Quebec, or whether to implement a bilingual system. Nevertheless, any system must provide opportunities for Israeli Jewish and Palestinian children to learn and play together, and ultimately to get to know and trust each other as citizens of the same country.

Integration along the American model has largely failed. In the United States, school integration proceeded from the correct premise that each child has equal rights and must receive an adequate education regardless of the child's race or ethnicity. This necessary principle is insufficient to ensure equal chances in life and to educate students to become citizens who share common values and mutual respect. Children come from diverse cultural backgrounds and unless this is recognized and supported in the school context, the values and norms of one culture (usually that which has been or remains economically and politically dominant) will continue to marginalize and exclude children of other cultures, even if nominally all children have the same rights. In Israel-Palestine this would mean recognizing that Palestinian and Israeli Jewish children have distinct heritages and that their parents will want to see their own languages, cultures, and religions persist and flourish.

Innovative models exist. The European School of Brussels in Uccle, which I attended, is one such example. Founded in 1953 as the first of ten such schools now in operation throughout the European Union, the school was originally established to allow the children of functionaries of the New European Coal and Steel Community (the forerunner of the EU) to be educated in their own languages. The school uses a curriculum that is in effect the highest common denominator of the national curricula of each of the member states and is taught in all the languages of the European Union. Each student belongs to a language section in which she is taught basic courses like literature and writing, mathematics, and the sciences. It is normal to study at least two additional languages. In the secondary grades, courses like history and geography, music, art, and physical education are taught in a second language. The miracle of the school is that it creates a situation where everyone understands what it means to be in a minority. Every child gains the experience of mixing with others as the norm, not the exception, and on the whole, the system works.

In fact, something similar is already being attempted in Israel. Established in 1997, the Hand in Hand schools challenge the highly segregated society in which Jewish and Arab Israelis live by creating institutions that are bilingual and integrated. Jewish and Arab children learn side by side in classrooms teamtaught by two teachers, one Arab and one Israeli Jewish. Each teacher speaks exclusively in his or her mother tongue, "assuring that pupils' primary linguistic role model is a native speaker."[26] The schools attempt to take this classroom dynamic and extend it to the wider community by involving the children's families in decision making and hosting programs to promote coexistence, including lectures, film series, language classes, dialogue groups, and holiday events. As challenging as the schools' mission has been, a reflection from a parent who was a member of the school steering committee inspires hope: "[I]ntegration has been difficult, but it has always been easier for the children than for the adults."[27] The Hand in Hand schools started with one site and fifty children; by 2006, there were three schools with nearly seven hundred children, and the program continues to grow rapidly. These efforts can also benefit from lessons learned from initiatives to integrate schools in Northern Ireland.[28] Such initiatives demonstrate that Palestinian-Israeli, and Muslim, Christian, and Jewish cooperation, which existed in Palestine's past, can be re-created in the future. There would be no better way to produce peace and justice than to teach our children how to practice it toward each other, and by demonstrating it toward them by ending the disparities in the current situation.

Multicultural and multireligious societies face particular challenges constituting legal systems. The principle of equality before the law suggests the need for a uniform legal code. In practice, many countries, including Israel, Jordan, and India, have mixed legal systems. There is a uniform criminal and civil law and an independent judiciary to which all persons are subject. However, when it comes to matters of "personal status," such as marriage, divorce, adoption, and inheritance, different religious communities often apply their own systems. In India, for example, Muslims and Christians have their own laws covering these matters, while Hindus, Sikhs, Buddhists, and others apply a version of Hindu law. This system was inherited from the colonial period, and after India gained independence, its constitution included the goal of eventually establishing a "uniform civil code." In practice, Indians have preferred the status quo because the prospect of change remains highly contentious. Similar systems, bequeathed by former imperial rulers, exist in Jordan and the occupied territories for Muslims and Christians, and in Israel for Muslims, Christians, and Jews. Given the long-standing acceptance of such mixed systems dealing with personal status among both Israelis and Palestinians, there is a case for continuity, rather than immediately seeking radical change. However, there has long been agitation within the Israeli Jewish secular majority against Orthodox Judaism's monopoly over control of personal status issues. It is not inconceivable to imagine Jews, Muslims, and Christians forming a joint constituency of reform in this area, particularly with respect to women's rights.

Can we also imagine new symbols with which the communities in the country, once bitterly at odds, can all identify? It will take time and effort for such symbols to evolve. The temporary flag for the new South Africa, which incorporated the symbolic colors of the country's different communities, including the orange of the Afrikaners, proved so popular that it was adopted permanently. Palestinians and Israelis will have to create such symbols of their own. To take one example, May 15, the date in 1948 that marked the end of the British Mandate, could be chosen as the day for a new constitution to become effective, a new beginning for everyone. Postapartheid South Africa, in another example, has adopted two national anthems.

And what will this country be called? Whenever I speak to an audience about one Palestinian-Israeli state, I know I have made a breakthrough when someone asks me that question. It means he has taken the leap to thinking about the practical realities and is imagining a common future. The reality regarding names is that "Israel" and "Palestine" are dear to those who use them and they should not be abandoned. The country could be called Yisrael-Falastin in Hebrew and Filastin-Isra'il in Arabic. We shall just have to toss a coin to decide whether "Israel" or "Palestine" will come first in the English version of the name. In day-to-day speech, people will most likely say "Israel" or "Palestine," as they do now, but in all official documents and pronouncements and in parliament, the joint name could be used. Perhaps in time, when a more common identity has developed, some other term will emerge.

All this is a sketch, a suggestion for a shared future for Israelis and Palestinians in a society that is democratic and tolerant, where two peoples who have fought for decades agree on rules that all can live by. There is no end of reasons to be skeptical that either group can ever be convinced to follow such a path. Where then can we find hope? There is some hope among some Israelis and Palestinians, and I will explore that. But first, I want to look at South Africa, an example of a country where two groups who had fought each other to a stalemate and were staring into the abyss of endless civil war chose an amazing path of reconciliation.

CHAPTER FIVE

Learning from South Africa

On May 10, 1994, watching Nelson Mandela take the oath as president of South Africa, F. W. de Klerk, the outgoing president of the apartheid regime, reflected on his Afrikaner ancestors. "The dream they had dreamt of being free and separate people, with their own right to national self-determination in their own national state in southern Africa" was, de Klerk recounted, "the ideal to which I myself had clung until I finally concluded, after a long process of deep introspection, that, if pursued, it would bring disaster to all the peoples of our country, including my own."[1] The ability of white South Africans to make this once unthinkable transition prevented an endless civil war. What made the change much easier was that the African National Congress (ANC), headed by Nelson Mandela, simultaneously led the internal and global resistance to apartheid and white minority rule, while constructively addressing white fears about the postapartheid future.

Drawing parallels between Israel-Palestine and apartheid South Africa makes some people very uncomfortable, as I learned a few years ago when I spoke on a panel with Rabbi Arnold

Wolf, a highly regarded Chicago community leader and early proponent of a Palestinian state among liberal American Jews. I compared arguments that were made to shield Israel from international criticism to those used to justify the actions of apartheid South Africa. Wolf was incensed. "The analogy is despicable," he roared. "The situation was never like it was in South Africa."[2] His reaction is not surprising. Mandela himself observed that with the exception of Hitler's genocide against the Jews, "there is no evil that has been so condemned by the entire world as apartheid."[3] Few people, let alone Jewish supporters of Israel, want to be placed in the same league. Many liberal Zionists were active in the antiapartheid struggle and cannot accept that the Israel they love could have anything in common with the hated apartheid regime. But my purpose here is not to argue that Israel is or is not as bad as apartheid South Africa, nor to deny the differences between the two situations, but to consider a recent experience where people with fundamentally incompatible views of history, locked for centuries in a bitter conflict of unfathomable misery and suffering, could emerge in peaceful reconciliation. When asked what he might tell some visiting Israelis, Pik Botha, foreign minister during the apartheid regime, said, "We could explain how we overcame our own fear of majority rule and began to realize that majority rule was something in our interest in the long term." If the Israelis "are interested," Botha offered, "we can, in all humility, explain how we came to the point of transforming our society."[4] Can Israelis and Palestinians really afford not to learn all the lessons South Africa may hold?

* * *

The struggle against apartheid earned the support of the world because it was waged in the name of universal values. As a Palestinian, I identified with the antiapartheid struggle and yet saw beyond its universality specific elements that shed light on the situation in my own country. Zionist and Afrikaner histories, for example, reveal strong common themes of collective identities shaped by memories of expulsion, persecution, redemption, and rebirth and guided by a single-minded quest for national survival. To both Zionists and Afrikaners it is not clear why their view of history and the conclusions they draw from it are not self-evident to the rest of the world. Understanding the motivations of Afrikaners allowed me to gain a certain empathy for Zionists.

The origins of the Afrikaner identity date back to April 6, 1652, when the Dutch East India Company established a colony on the Cape of Good Hope at the southern tip of Africa. Nelson Mandela explains that April 6 was "the day white South Africans annually commemorate[d] the founding of their country—and Africans revile[d] as the beginning of three hundred years of enslavement."[5] This anniversary is redolent of May 14, the day in 1948 that Israel declared independence but which Palestinians observe as *al-nakba*—the catastrophe—the beginning of their exile and subjugation. In the late seventeenth century, colonists arrived at the cape from the Netherlands, Germany, France, and other parts of Europe, many escaping appalling religious persecution and massacres in their home countries. In the 1830s, the Afrikaners or Boers (as these colonists eventually called themselves), chafing under British rule and in search of more land, set off to conquer the interior. These arduous journeys on foot and in covered wagons became known as the Great Treks and ended with the establishment of three independent republics. During the Boer Wars in the late 1800s and early 1900s, the British crushed the Boer republics, generating enduring Afrikaner bitterness. The "Anglo-Boer War burnt itself into the collective consciousness of my people, the Afrikaners, like no other event in our history," de Klerk has said. The British scorched-earth policy destroyed farms and killed livestock, and ended Boer independence. Worst of all, the British "interned our women and children in what became known as concentration camps." (The term "concentration camp" was first used in this context.) Of the entire Afrikaner population—a few hundred thousand at the time— tens of thousands are believed to have died in the camps.[6]

Afrikaners were determined never again to submit to foreign rule or forgo their independence and security. In 1910, the predominantly British-settled colonies of the cape and the former Boer republics in the interior formed the Union of South Africa, which excluded all indigenous African peoples, as well as Indians and other Asians, from any political power. Then, when the Afrikaner-dominated National Party won the whites-only general election in 1948, they ushered in a new era of more formalized discrimination—apartheid. As Mandela observes, the 1948 Nationalist election victory was, in the "cosmology" of Afrikaners, "like the Israelites' journey to the Promised Land. This was the fulfillment of God's promise, and the justification for their view that South Africa should be a white man's country forever."[7] Afrikaners themselves compared the Great Treks to the Israelites' exodus from Egypt, and saw their republics as a "new Israel," built in a land redeemed from godless "Canaanites."[8] Out of the undeniable suffering and trauma of the Boer Wars, Afrikaners constructed an ideology in which they were in a state of permanent victimhood. They acted with the belief that God was on their side in a struggle for self-preservation against external forces whose sole motivation was their destruction. Palestinians see a very similar process in Israel where, says Oren Yiftachel, a professor of political geography at Ben-Gurion University of the Negev, the "exclusively Jewish discourse" ignores the consequences of Zionist practices on the Palestinians, leaving the latter as a kind of "silent backdrop or incidental stage setting" to a drama that is seen to have only Jewish protagonists. It is this blindness, in Yiftachel's view, that "allows most Jews to believe to this day the illusion that they have a 'Jewish democracy,' despite the apartheid reality that is created by Jewish rule before their very eyes."[9]

Yiftachel's point underscores that the national dramas of Zionists and Afrikaners were performed on stages—the territories of Palestine and South Africa—that were already occupied by other people who could fit into the national narratives of the ruling groups in only one of two ways: In the first, Africans and Arabs are seen as uncivilized peoples whose resistance to domination is irrational and motivated by hatred, thus vindicating the dominant group's sense of victimization; in the second, they are a welcoming and willingly subservient population grateful for the rationalism and superior technology brought by the newcomers. These views of indigenous peoples were common to Europeans who settled in North America and Australasia as well, but the near annihilation of the native populations in those places eliminated the need to grapple with the challenge posed by a significant or majority native community. Indeed, de Klerk is correct when he points out that at the time of the Boer Wars, "few people in Europe questioned the right of the brave 'Boers' to national self-determination." But in the emerging postcolonial world of the 1950s and 1960s—when human rights perspectives had displaced colonialist rationales—"hardly anyone any longer acknowledged this right," although it had been the driving force of Afrikaner politics throughout the first sixty years of the twentieth century."[10]

Both Zionists and Afrikaners responded to resistance from the native population by rhetorically reversing the colonial relationship and claiming that they, not Arabs or Africans, were the true indigenous people of the country. Their relationship to British colonial authorities helped bolster this belief. Traditional Zionist history presents Israel's 1947–48 war as an anticolonial struggle against the British. Before Israel was established, armed Zionist groups frequently attacked British forces and civilians in Palestine. The most deadly attack in this period occurred on July 22, 1946, when future Israeli prime minister Menachem Begin's Irgun organization bombed the British Mandate headquarters at the King David Hotel in Jerusalem, killing ninety-one people, the majority Arab, Jewish, and British civilians. British restrictions on Jewish immigration during the 1930s also helped feed Zionist antagonism. In the late 1950s and early 1960s, Israel consciously tried to win recognition in newly independent African states by claiming to be, like them, the product of an anticolonial struggle. Likewise, Afrikaners' deep bitterness toward the British simmered for decades after the formation of the Union of South Africa. But the reality is that in both instances, whatever antagonisms existed, neither Zionists nor Afrikaners would have gained control over their countries without the benefit of British power, which crushed and delegitimized indigenous resistance on their behalf.[11]

To the ears of Palestinians or Africans, the justifications of Zionist and Afrikaner pioneers presented a stark choice: Submit or disappear. When they refused to do either, conflict was inevitable. At the heart of both clashes is the fact that what Israeli Jews and white South Africans tried to erase from view always remained visible and alive to Palestinians and Africans. Nelson Mandela recalls a journey through South Africa in 1955 to organize African National Congress resistance:

> From Durban I drove south along the coast past Port Shepstone and Port St. Johns, small and lovely colonial towns that dotted the shimmering beaches fronting the Indian Ocean. While mesmerized by the beauty of the area, I was constantly rebuked by the buildings and streets that bear the names of white imperialists who suppressed the very people whose names belonged there.[12]

Mandela's observation is reminiscent of the famous statement the legendary general Moshe Dayan made in 1969, reviewing Israel's achievements in its first twenty years:

> Jewish villages were built in the place of Arab villages. You don't even know the names of these Arab villages, and I don't blame you, because these geography books no longer exist. Not only do the books not exist, the Arab

villages are not there either. Nahalal arose in the place of Mahlul, Gvat in the place of Jibta, Sarid in the place of Haneifa, and Kfar-Yehoshua in the place of Tel-Shaman. There is not one single place built in this country that did not have a former Arab population.[13]

Living in what amounts to a self-contained moral universe in which the victors are the permanent victims and the "others" are invisible except as a threat allows Israel—as with apartheid South Africa—to justify to itself almost any measure. Both countries have depicted themselves as vulnerable outposts of Western civilization in "tough neighborhoods," with the clear implication that the normal rules observed with more "civilized" neighbors are a luxury they could not afford.

This shared mentality of survival justifying any means led to Israel being the closest ally of apartheid South Africa when it was most isolated internationally. Although Israel kept its distance officially, it helped South Africa circumvent international sanctions, engaged in brisk trade, and provided technological know-how.[14] For decades, Israel played a "crucial role in the survival of the apartheid regime," according to Israeli scholar Benjamin Beit-Hallahmi,[15] breaking the international arms boycott to become South Africa's main foreign arms supplier. The most significant area of cooperation was that Israel helped the apartheid regime to develop nuclear weapons.[16]

The similarity between some of their own policies and Israel's was not lost on apartheid planners, as an incident recounted by Meron Benvenisti reveals. "I was invited with a colleague of mine, one of [Moshe] Dayan's advisers on the West Bank, to lunch with a South African official on a visit to Jerusalem," Benvenisti recalled. "During lunch, we discussed our work, and the visitor showed great interest in our ideas on how to improve Israeli-Palestinian relations by leaving the Palestinians alone to manage their own affairs. Suddenly he said, 'How would you react if we were to invite you to advise the new regime in Transkei?' We were shocked. His query implied that he considered our work comparable with their reactionary, racist schemes in the Bantustans. When we expressed our indignation, he smiled and said, 'I understand your reaction. But aren't we actually doing the same thing? We are faced with the same existential problem, therefore we arrive at the same solution.'"[17]

Today, de Klerk grapples with a conundrum: "My father was a good and kind man. So were all—or most—of his colleagues that came to our home while I was growing up, whose children I knew at school and university. How could he—how could we all—have supported policies that we now regard as unjust and oppressive?"[18] The civilized face that apartheid South Africa sought to present, including parliamentary democracy, an advanced and scientific economy, immaculate towns with lush gardens framing monuments to its pioneering heroes, was paid for by the people living in the squalid townships, crowded into tin shacks, surrounded by open sewers, robbed of freedom, opportunity, health, and dignity, and kept in place through dehumanizing brutality. The struggle to hide this reality from the world and from their own people became for apartheid rulers an all-consuming preoccupation, requiring ever greater deceptions and violence.

But things don't necessarily start off this way. Afrikaner nationalists had what were in their own eyes defensible and moral motivations for their policies, bending liberal principles to decidedly illiberal ends. "Foremost among these," says de Klerk, reaching into the separate moral universe of Afrikaner nationalism, "was our conviction that without apartheid, our people would be swamped by the vast black majority—and that this would inevitably lead to the extinction of our own hard-won right to national self-determination."[19] Undoubtedly a sincere reflection of the prevailing Afrikaner state of mind, de Klerk's words echo precisely the justifications so frequently heard for the essential need for a Jewish state: A small minority that has survived near extinction longs only for a place to be safe, to be alone with itself.

By the time de Klerk became president, decades of experience had shown him that Afrikaner ideals "could be clung to only by withholding justice from other South Africans and by denying the economic and demographic realities of the country."[20] "The most important lesson that emerged from our experience in South Africa is that no vision of the future can justify any government to ignore the basic human rights of the human beings involved."[21] De Klerk recognized that the Afrikaner rationale could not survive. Israeli leaders too seem to understand that Zionism operates in a separate moral universe. As Jewish settlers were removed from Gaza in August 2005, Shimon Peres explained, "We are disengaging from Gaza because of demography." Responding to Peres's statement,

Israeli commentator Daphna Baram remarked, "The desire to maintain a Jewish majority in Israel is seen by most Jewish Israelis as a liberal aspiration, rather than a racist one, as it would appear elsewhere."[22] For now, Israelis like Peres seem untroubled by the jarring dissonance between their liberal self-perception and the reality of their policies. But the implication of the South African experience is that one day the world might view Israeli Jews' claim to separateness, so right and natural within their own justifications, as something that cannot be attained without unacceptable violations of Palestinian rights. The hope held out by South Africa is that when Israelis and Palestinians finally do conclude that separation is unachievable, there is an example of an alternative to perpetual conflict.

To F. W. de Klerk, the Road Map, the U.S.-sponsored peace plan that is supposed to lead to the creation of a Palestinian state, looked exactly like the plan for "grand apartheid" that South African prime minister Hendrik Verwoerd set in motion in the mid-1950s. "The idea was originally sound," de Klerk maintains; "as a young parliamentarian I was enthusiastic about forming independent homelands for every group, including the Afrikaners. . . . The roadmap between Israel and Palestine," in de Klerk's analysis, "is based on exactly the same principles."[23] As he observed, "[W]hat apartheid originally wanted to achieve is what everybody now says is the solution for Israel and Palestine, namely—partitioning, separate nation states on the bases of ethnicity, different cultures, different languages."[24]

The basic principle behind grand apartheid was that whites would preserve and normalize their power by manipulating the demographics and political boundaries of South Africa to create "independent" black states. All blacks would be given citizenship in these states and therefore, the apartheid planners thought, they could forestall demands for blacks to vote in South Africa. Grand apartheid offered de Klerk's generation "what we imagined would be a moral solution to our complex problems because it would assure the rights of all South Africa's people—including our own—to self-determination and political rights within their own areas."[25] It was a bold attempt to make the Afrikaner nationalist moral universe merge with the values of apartheid's critics by disguising the status quo of white dominance as black independence. Millions of blacks were forced to move to the Bantustans, while large cities were reserved for whites. The "independent" Bantustans (five out of a planned ten were set up) had flags and armies of their own, but were totally subsidized by South Africa. Several had military dictators and were corrupt. The apartheid regime repeatedly proposed to free Nelson Mandela from prison if he would recognize the Transkei Bantustan and move there, but he dismissed what he termed "an offer only a turncoat could accept."[26] Indeed, it has become increasingly common for Palestinians to refer to the "state" that Israel may be prepared to grant them in small, disconnected, walled-in ghettos as a "Bantustan." One can't help contrasting the courage and principle of Mandela, who preferred to stay in prison rather than grant legitimacy to the Bantustans, and the desperate, foolish, self-serving decision of Yasser Arafat to accept Israel's conditions as a tinpot ruler of a Transkei on the Mediterranean.

Resistance to apartheid stiffened as rioting and violence turned widespread, as thousands of nonwhites were killed, imprisoned, and tortured, and as South Africa's isolation grew.

Some Afrikaners like de Klerk acknowledged that there was only one way out of the impasse.[27] Whites had to overcome their "fear of black domination" and agree to negotiate with the ANC whom they had for decades vilified as a revolutionary terrorist organization bent on their destruction. This embattled and fearful community of four million South African whites was "riding the tiger of growing black anger and increasing international isolation." They faced the world and thirty-five million black South Africans who "were shouting at white South Africans to dismount."[28] The problem for a minority that had been in power and caused so much suffering for so long was that it was "difficult for them to see how they could do so without being devoured." "For white South Africans," de Klerk said in 2004,

> acceptance of a one-man, one-vote solution evoked very much the same fears and reaction that could be expected from Israelis were they ever asked to consign their fate to a one-man, one-vote election in a greater Israel/Palestine in which they would be heavily outnumbered.[29]

Whites were able to dismount without being devoured because the ANC was ready with a vision that allowed them to do so. The ANC had always been clear and consistent in its stand against partition of South Africa and a black nationalist state in favor of democracy. The Freedom Charter adopted by the ANC and its allies in 1955 put forward a progressive vision of a nonracial country that held that "South Africa belongs to all who live in it, black and white." This vision, while challenged by black nationalists, gained the support of the majority of black South Africans, uniting them with Indians and "coloreds" as well as liberal and communist whites.

There is a crucial contrast here with the Palestinian national movement, which until the 1980s also opposed partition. But it was never able to build a consensus around a clear, simple, and inclusive alternative like the Freedom Charter as Palestinians were unable to reconcile themselves to the presence of millions of Israeli Jews. Palestinians had no clear answer for what ought to happen to Israeli Jews, some hinting that they might be allowed to stay, while others suggested that all but those with roots predating the Zionist movement would have to leave. This inability to see how Israelis could fit into a just vision of the future is perhaps explained by the freshness of the Palestinian trauma. Whereas most Jews had arrived in Palestine in the three decades immediately prior to 1948, whites had been in South Africa for three centuries.

Most Palestinians, like black nationalists, saw themselves caught in a conflict between settlers and natives who could not coexist. Israel's refusal to allow any refugees to return sent the clearest message to Palestinians that either they or Israeli Jews could inhabit the land but not both. The goal of black nationalists in South Africa, according to Mahmoud Mamdani, a leading Africanist scholar, "was to rid the land of settlers who sought political power to undergird a privileged position in the economy and society."[30] The Palestinian national movement tended to resemble the minority black nationalist position rather than that of the ANC. The only real evolution has been over who is a settler. Until the 1960s, most Palestinians saw all Israelis as settlers to be driven from the entirety of Palestine. Gradually, Palestinians have come to terms with the presence of Israelis and now express a willingness to limit the term "settler" only to those in the West Bank and East Jerusalem. The majority would be content to see them move out of these areas so Palestinians could establish a nationalist state that would mirror Zionist nationalism across the border.

The ANC's breakthrough was its ability to transcend narrow nationalism. In the ANC's view, as Mamdani explains:

The problem was not the settler but the settler state, the legal setup that guaranteed settler privilege. Without a state that legally discriminated between settler and native, there would be no settler privilege and, thus, no settler, since all settlers would become as immigrants whose historical origins would cease to have significance in law. The enemy from this point of view was everyone who defended the power of the settler state. Instead of embracing the mirror image of settler ideology—by turning the identity of "native" from a racial stigma into a badge of racial pride—the promise of postapartheid South Africa was to let go of both "settler" and "native" as twin political identities generated by the settler state. As the ANC put it so subversively in its Freedom Charter, South Africa belongs to all those who live in it.[31]

Mandela accepted Afrikaners' claims that they were true Africans, which often put him at odds with black nationalists. He did observe, however, that "the Afrikaner had stoutly defended his independence against British imperialism and struck a blow for nationalism. Now the descendants of those same freedom fighters were persecuting my people who were struggling for precisely the same thing the Afrikaners had once fought and died for."[32] Mandela was able to accept his enemy's narrative without compromising on the demand that Afrikaners relinquish their exclusive claim on power. Mandela urged South Africans to embrace any Afrikaner who abandoned apartheid, and thus Afrikaners gained a legitimacy in the eyes of other South Africans that they were unable to wrest through centuries of domination. It is an incredibly simple and powerful maneuver, yet one that so far has been beyond the ability of most Israelis and Palestinians. "From a postapartheid point of view," Mamdani concludes, "the real issue in Palestine and Israel is not whether there should be one, two or ten states but how to base any state on equal citizenship for all who live in it."[33] Palestinian thinkers, among them Azmi Bishara and Joseph Massad, have made similar points.[34] This is, of course, correct: The moment Israelis and Palestinians commit themselves to full equality, there is no rationale for separate states.

Even with such a commitment, the practicalities of giving up power are still daunting. The demographic imbalance between rulers and ruled is not nearly as dramatic in Palestine-Israel as in South Africa, where blacks outnumber whites by about eight to one. Within historic Palestine, Jews are now only barely a minority, though if the refugees outside the country are taken into account, Palestinians outnumber Israeli Jews by about two to one. The vast numerical superiority of blacks was an inescapable reality for the apartheid rulers. Israeli Jews may feel that their relative strength in numbers means they can continue to resist demographic reality. Yet at the same time, the numerical disadvantage of white South Africans surely made the prospect of dismounting the tiger of black anger that much more terrifying. They too had been raised for generations to believe that any surrender of control would lead not only to economic and political loss, but even to extermination.[35]

The multiparty negotiations to create a new constitution for South Africa were difficult and faced many near-fatal crises but in the end they yielded a constitution with a strong Bill of Rights, with a guarantee of the right to education in the language of a person's choice and a legal affirmation of the Freedom Charter's promise that "South Africa belongs to all who live in it, united in our diversity." Nelson Mandela understood that white fears boiled down to visceral human concerns that the ANC had to address if transformation was to be achieved peacefully. "During the transition" to democracy, he told white South Africans, "[M]inorities everywhere will say: 'If the change comes, what is going to happen to me, to my spouse, to my children, to the national group to which I belong, to the values in which I believe, to my possessions?' "[36] Mandela reassured white South Africans that "[w]e do not want to drive you into the sea"[37] and became, in the words of Nadine Gordimer, the "personification of the future,"[38] delivering a message that reconciliation was possible because it would be accompanied by economic and social transformation. An example of the practical ways in which Mandela's reassurances were institutionalized came when the ANC agreed to honor all existing civil service contracts, assuring white administrators and middle managers of their personal security in the immediate future, while guaranteeing the continuity of basic services under the ANC, which had no previous experience of government. Although whites once voted by overwhelming margins in favor of the apartheid program put forward by the National Party, 69 percent of whites voted in favor of the National Party's program to abandon apartheid in a 1992 referendum. Few heeded the nationalist siren song of the far right who wanted to fight to the bitter end.[39] What was once unthinkable to most whites became reality with their consent.

An inclusive vision and a generous spirit are essential requirements for reconciliation, but they are clearly insufficient. For decades, the white government of South Africa simply dismissed the Freedom Charter and claimed that the ANC's true intentions were not democracy but dictatorship and vengeance. It was only when internal and external pressure made the monopoly on power too costly to maintain that whites grasped for a way out and listened seriously to the ANC's ideas. Hence, continued resistance and struggle to raise the cost of the status quo for the powerful party is also essential. But a delicate balance requires that resistance exacts a price yet avoids creating so much new suffering that reconcilation becomes impossible. For resistance movements like the antiapartheid coalition or for the Palestinians, the question of where, when, and how violence fits in is often central and highly fraught.

On coming to office, de Klerk believed that superior military force alone could allow the white government to retain power for another ten years, but only at the cost of inflicting enormous casualties.[40] A different leader might have decided to fight on at all costs and de Klerk's strongest opponents among white South Africans wanted to do exactly that. De Klerk had absorbed that "the struggle could not be won by brutal, unconventional operations which were in conflict with common decency and basic morality." Looking back on the regime's long history of repression, de Klerk concluded that "there is no evidence that the assassination of opponents had the slightest effect on the final outcome of the struggle—other than causing further personal suffering and bitterness."[41] Mandela too had concluded that a military victory for the liberation movement "was a distant if not impossible dream" and that the only outcome from continued fighting would be thousands or even millions of deaths.[42] Mandela understood, and convinced the ANC leadership, that each side in the struggle could through violence deny victory to the other but not ensure that it would prevail.[43]

The ANC did not give up its right to armed struggle until well after Mandela had been released and negotiations begun with the government. Throughout his years in prison, he maintained that the ANC was right to turn to armed struggle, and would be justified in using "terrorism" if sabotage and guerrilla warfare failed to yield results.[44] Mandela defended his decision to abandon nonviolence in the early 1960s, "for it had done nothing to stem the violence of the state nor change the heart of our oppressors."[45] In Mandela's analysis, "[I]t is always the oppressor, not the oppressed, who dictates the form of the struggle. If the oppressor uses violence, the oppressed have no alternative but to respond violently."[46] Yet violence was never the main feature of the antiapartheid struggle. Even though the ANC did occasionally kill white South Africans in spectacular bombings, its violence was often more symbolic and wielded more effectively as a threat than a campaign.

Neither Israelis nor Palestinians, despite decades of bloodshed, have reached de Klerk's and Mandela's conclusion. There can be few who still seriously believe they can totally defeat the other side by force of arms, yet significant groups on both sides remain committed to fighting. As Israel rushed to complete the colonization of the West Bank in the 1990s, its chief excuse for lack of peace was always "Palestinian violence." Indeed, the phenomenon of Palestinian suicide bombers appeared at precisely the time—the year after the Oslo Accords were signed—that Israel began its greatest-ever settlement drive. Suicide bombings reached their peak in 2001–3 as Israel moved to crush the Palestinian uprising, killing thousands of unarmed civilians and injuring tens of thousands of others. Among Palestinians and in the broader Arab world, opinion on the use of the tactic was sharply split. Some saw attacks on civilians as the only means Palestinians had to puncture the immunity Israel enjoyed by virtue of its vast military superiority. Others viewed bombs on buses and in cafés as morally unacceptable, arguing as well that they compromised the integrity of the Palestinian cause in the eyes of those whose assistance Palestinians needed.

This debate started the day after the first suicide attack against Israeli civilians, in Afula, on April 6, 1994. The *New York Times* reported on reactions among Palestinians. "I feel sorry for them, but they should feel what we feel," said a schoolgirl in Ramallah, articulating a pragmatic line. "[T]hey're killing us every day. We walk down the street, and at any second something can happen to us. This reminded them that if you kill people, you're going to get killed." A woman from the village of Qarawat Bani Zayd expressed moral opposition: "This is an unacceptable crime. Our leadership has to condemn it, and the people as well. We feel for the victims and for their families." An eleventh-grade boy supported the bombing: "This is not terrorism. It is a war. An eye for an eye. What he [the bomber] did cannot be worse than what that guy [Baruch Goldstein] did in Hebron." Interestingly, though, the *Times* found that "few people echoed those words of support, though many were reluctant to condemn the attack."[47] In the years since 1994, opinion polls have shown Palestinian support swinging from majorities in favor of such attacks to majorities strongly opposed, usually with approval rising as Palestinians feel more hopeless.[48] What might this ambiguity mean, and what opportunity does it offer? Again, South Africa suggests an important lesson.

There is a strong similarity between the debate over suicide attacks and the discussion during the antiapartheid struggle about necklacing—the practice of setting fire to a gasoline-filled tire placed around the neck of suspected collaborators or sometimes even their relatives or associates. Thousands of South Africans, including children, were killed in this grisly way. "As with suicide bombing," Mamdani observed, "the debate on necklacing also had two sides to it. Its moral side often sounded less like a critique of necklacing than a settler discourse on the lack of civilization among natives: What kind of society would countenance such a practice? In contrast, the debate among natives—in the ranks of the liberation movements—was more often than not about the political effectiveness of necklacing in checking the proliferation of informers."[49] In 1985, Winnie Mandela made a highly publicized speech praising necklacing. The ANC was reluctant to repudiate her words despite international pressure. The organization's exiled leader, Oliver Tambo, said only, "[W]e are not happy with the necklace but we will not condemn people who have been driven to adopt such extremes."[50] Palestinians found themselves split between similar sentiments. For the first time, suicide bombing changed the calculus faced by Israeli leaders, and many Palestinians were reluctant to forgo the power it gave them over their oppressors even if they could not fully embrace the method.

In South Africa, as in Palestine-Israel, the powerful side chose to judge the weak through a moral lens while, of course, exempting its own violence from such scrutiny; a majority of Israelis routinely accept their government's rationale for violence against Palestinians without question. However, anyone who discusses suicide attacks by Palestinians as a political phenomenon, rather than a cultural-moral or religious defect, will quickly find herself accused of condoning terrorism. Jenny Tonge, a British member of Parliament, discovered this for herself in January 2004 after she stated that she could understand how a Palestinian might choose to become a suicide bomber, given the brutal conditions of life under Israeli occupation. Tonge lost her job as spokesperson for her party, the Liberal Democrats, and was accused by leaders of providing "justification" for suicide bombing, something she emphatically denied.[51] Tonge paid dearly for challenging the approach that denies that rational people, who would usually never dream of killing, can be driven to do horrible things under oppressive conditions, but to move the discussion forward we need to do just that. A groundbreaking study by University of Chicago political scientist Robert Pape called *Dying to Win*, examining all suicide attacks worldwide since 1980 (460 were included in the study), revealed that every such bombing campaign had a clear goal that was secular and political: to compel a modern democracy to withdraw military forces from territory that the suicide attackers viewed as their homeland.

In South Africa, the political debate on necklacing "had to go beyond the question of the immediate effectiveness" of the practice "to probe its longer-run political costs," among them "alienating allies, both at home and abroad," and fostering "growing militarism in the culture of resistance."[52] Mamdani discerns two lessons of immediate relevance to Israel-Palestine. The first is that "so long as there was no effective political alternative, it was difficult to discredit necklacing politically. Once a nonviolent way of ending apartheid appeared as an alternative, it was as if the sun had come up, the fog lifted, and there was a new dawn; in a land where few had dared even to whisper criticism only yesterday, hardly anyone could be found to champion necklacing the day after."[53] The quickest way to end support for violence against Israeli civilians would be for the international community to provide an alternative, primarily in the form of external pressure on Israel that exacts a high price for its oppression of Palestinians. Failing that, Palestinians and their allies need, morally and strategically, to turn to resistance that maximizes pressure on Israel without killing innocent civilians, capitalizes on global support, mobilizes the greatest number of people, and does not foreclose the possibility of future reconciliation. The international antiapartheid movement combined economic sanctions, an arms embargo, and a sporting and cultural boycott. While the ANC employed armed struggle, it focused on sabotage and military targets and wielded it more effectively as a threat than a full-blown reality.

As in South Africa, the total elimination of violence in a situation of conflict is impossible. Like Israel, the white government of South Africa always insisted that it would not negotiate as long as violence continued. Of course, it defined its enemies' acts as "violence" and "terrorism," while its own actions were considered part of "maintaining law and order" or "urban planning." Once the apartheid rulers understood that violence would only escalate in the absence of good-faith negotiations, they dropped this convenient excuse not to talk. "We negotiated under fire," de Klerk recalls. "South Africa was burning with violence, but no one allowed himself the luxury of believing that we could wait with the negotiations until the violence ceased."[54]

The clearest lesson from South Africa's example is that the Palestinian message and methods must make it clear that the target is not the Israeli people but an unjust system that denies one people their rights, identity, and dignity, and condemns the other to increasing isolation, fear, and moral corruption. The movement should not be framed around Palestinian nationalism, but should call for a democracy that will protect all people and emancipate them from the prison of communal interest and competition. While building international pressure against the current system and exacting a price from those who support it, Palestinians need to articulate a vision of the future in which Israelis can see themselves. While undoubtedly unfair that Palestinians should shoulder the burden of reassurance when they have disproportionately borne the costs of the conflict, it is a fact that the oppressed must often show their oppressors a way out of the hole they have dug. What Palestinians can learn from South Africa is that the promise of a future of reconciliation rather than revenge can rob an unjust system of the support it needs to survive because such systems are often built on fear—in the case of Israel and South Africa, the fear, stoked by politicians, of being destroyed. The lesson for Israelis is to listen to their enemies rather than demonize them, which may lead to a secure future free of the burden of ruling others by force. They will gain the legitimacy and acceptance they have long craved, not just among Palestinians, but in the wider Arab and Muslim world.

South Africa's experience more than a decade after the end of apartheid demonstrates that reconciliation in a deeply divided society is difficult, painful, and vulnerable to constant setbacks. Attitudes change slowly. The suffering caused by apartheid has left deep scars. Economic and social inequalities entrenched by centuries of exploitation and discrimination cannot be undone at a stroke; they continue to rob people of their potential long after the dismantling of formal apartheid. Many black South Africans feel that too many of those responsible for apartheid policies escaped direct accountability, while many whites persist in denying the horror of apartheid. Some blacks feel that whites have resisted the faster economic change that would reduce the vast economic inequalities, while whites chafe at losing privileges as affirmative-action programs take effect.

While coping with the vast challenges of postapartheid reconciliation, South Africa has not had the luxury of immunity from all the other problems faced by the region. In the past decade, South Africa was hit hard by the Asian economic crisis, and it has had to confront the same forces of economic globalization that have reduced the sovereignty of so many national governments. More important, South Africa has been devastated by HIV/AIDS. And yet, for all these obstacles, the great majority of South Africans from every ethnic group remain committed to working for national reconciliation and unity.[55]

South Africans struggled hard to negotiate a constitutional dispensation all could live with and defend. Palestinians and Israelis would of course face similar challenges and others all their own. The bitterness and mistrust that both peoples feel is vast. The Palestinian experience—both historical and day to day—is a source of burning, urgent injustice and outrage. The anguish felt by Israelis for their losses can be no less intense than the pain of Palestinians. But can anyone say that the suffering and tragedy of Palestine-Israel have been greater or more profoundly felt than those of South Africa?

If Nelson Mandela is right that no evil other than the Nazi holocaust has been so unanimously condemned by the world as apartheid, then shouldn't we be inspired by the reconciliation, however halting and as yet incomplete, that has been possible between apartheid's victims and its perpetrators? Allister Sparks, the legendary editor of the antiapartheid *Rand Daily Mail* newspaper, observed that the conflict in his country most resembled those in Nothern Ireland and Palestine-Israel, because each involved "two ethno-nationalisms" in a seemingly irreconcilable rivalry for the "same piece of territory." If the prospect of "one secular country shared by all" seems "unthinkable" in Palestine-Israel, he says, then it is possible to appreciate how unlikely such a solution once looked in South Africa. But, "that is what we did," Sparks says, "without any foreign negotiator [and] no handshakes on the White House lawn."[56] The constitution of the new South Africa enshrines as a principle a "need for understanding but not for vengeance, a need for reparation but not retaliation, a need for *ubuntu* but not for victimisation."[57] And if South Africans are able to believe in this and work for it, there is no logical reason why Israelis and Palestinians cannot do the same. Taking the road that South Africa took may be the only way forward. The longer we wait before starting on it, the harder the path will be. It is not, to be sure, a road that leads to utopia, but only perhaps to the chance of a new beginning where we still would have to face the constant challenges of building a just, equitable, and tolerant society. When South Africans embarked on their journey, they had no guide. Palestinians and Israelis, at least, would have the chance to talk to South Africans, to learn from them and with them how to heal their terrible wounds, those they inherited and those that continue to be inflicted with every passing day.

CHAPTER SIX

Israelis and Palestinians Thinking the Unthinkable

I have argued that a successful strategy for democratic transformation in Israel-Palestine will in part require Palestinians to present a vision that meets the concerns and needs of ordinary Israeli Jews, alongside a principled and sustained campaign to impose a cost for Israeli government abuses of Palestinians. There is, however small, some existing debate among Palestinians and Israelis on a united democratic state. Any next steps involve concrete efforts to amplify that debate, along with an organized global campaign to support Palestinian rights.

Michael Tarazi, a legal adviser to the PLO, caused a stir when he published an op-ed in the *New York Times* in October 2004 warning that realities on the ground were forcing Palestinians to consider a one-state solution seriously. He observed that polls indicated the level of Palestinian support for the idea was "surprisingly high," given that the one-state solution is not officially advocated by any senior Palestinian leader."[1] Predictably, Tarazi's piece produced outraged responses claiming that the article proved the PLO had never given up its intention of "destroying Israel." More interesting was the response Tarazi got from Palestinians.

After the article appeared, Tarazi says he was contacted by several leaders of the Palestinian Authority who said words to the effect, "Michael, you're right, but we can't say that." Publicly, Tarazi observes, there is very little discussion of a one-state solution among Palestinians. Officials occasionally declare that Israel is making a two-state solution impossible, but they "won't take the next logical step" and talk about one state. When they do, as former P.A. prime minister Ahmed Qureia famously did in January 2004, "They use it more like a threat," Tarazi says, "which doesn't carry a whole lot of credibility with the Israelis." No Palestinian leader seems ready, Tarazi says, to "start confronting the sacred cow and saying, 'Wait a minute, we got it all wrong, maybe the age of nation-states has passed us by, so let's jump to the next phase.'"[2] Ali Jarbawi, a professor of political science at Birzeit University, says, "Most Palestinians prefer the idea of separation, because they want their own state." But Israel's "idea of a two-state solution is to squeeze us into cantons" and therefore, argues Jarbawi, "[g]iven a choice between cantonization and one state, Palestinians will go for the latter."[3] Support for a two-state solution among Palestinians in the occupied territories has hovered between 37 percent and 55 percent in recent years, while support for a "bi-national state in all of historic Palestine" has varied between one-quarter and one-third, according to surveys taken by the Jerusalem Media & Communications Centre (JMCC).[4]

There are good logical reasons to believe that a majority of Palestinians could come to see their future lying in a single, democratic state, sharing power equitably with Israeli Jews. Palestinians would gain access to political power and resources that they are currently being unfairly denied. Most Palestinians understand that what lies behind the conflict and violence is injustice, and healing this injustice is the only means to end the violence and dissipate the accumulated feelings of bitterness. Above all, a single state would mean reunification of Palestinians on both sides of the 1967 lines, and with those outside the country.

As the disparities between those with rights and those without become more glaring every day, ordinary Palestinians are being pushed by their own experiences to view the conflict more in terms of individual rights than national rights—and this is more noticeable in the countryside than among Palestinian opinion makers. "The Ramallah elite is very smug in its cafés and their houses are not being taken, their lives are not being disrupted the same way" as those directly in the path of the wall and the settlements, Tarazi says. "It hit home to me when I was in the Qalqilya region," Tarazi explains, "and I came across a farmer who was staring out at the other side of the wall and there was a highway where settlers were able to go. We started talking and he said, 'I don't care anymore about the Palestinian flag. I don't care anymore about the word "Palestine." I don't care anymore about the symbols. I just want to have the same rights as those settlers across the street. I want to be able to drive down this road, I want to be able to send my kids to the hospital or go on vacation when I want to go on vacation.'" Amira Hass of *Ha'aretz* confirms that Israel's measures, especially its movement restrictions, "privatized and individualized occupation."[5] The impact of the closures, curfews, and walls is collective, Hass explains, but Palestinians "experience it individually. You go to get a permit," and when it's denied, "you think it's something wrong with you or some mistake in the computer about you." Palestinians confront the daily problem of how to cope with closures affecting their work, livelihood, and childrens' educations in the absence of any Palestinian authority capable of providing relief or defending them against Israel's measures. Many Palestinian officials were isolated from these realities during the Oslo years as they possessed Israeli-issued VIP passes that allowed them to circumvent checkpoints, a source of resentment for ordinary people, who must line up for hours like cattle to pass through the turnstiles and gates set up by Israel. Hebron-based journalist Khaled Amayreh, who closely monitors public sentiment, concurs with Tarazi's observations: "I believe that the support for the one-state idea is more widespread among ordinary Palestinians than among intellectuals because ordinary people believe what they see, and what they see is that Israel and the West Bank are inextricably intertwined, even despite the gigantic annexation wall. Hence, the Palestinian masses are more likely to favor a one-state solution.[6]

This probability includes those Palestinians who voted for Hamas in the January 2006 Palestinian Authority legislative election, even though the election victory heightened Israeli fears of an Islamic state with the goal of destroying or expelling the Israeli Jewish community and fueled the call for fortified, unilateral separation. However, the vote for Hamas arose more from a Palestinian reaction to their worsening situation and despair than from a surge in religious fundamentalism. It is widely acknowledged that much of the Hamas vote was a protest against the endemic corruption and defeatism of the Fatah-led Palestinian Authority, which had neither provided good government nor made any progress in liberating Palestinians from Israeli occupation.

Voting for Hamas, which pointedly excluded its objectionable charter language from its election platform, was a way to defy what Palestinians saw as a corrupt "peace process," whereby foreign aid was traded for political concessions while Israel continued to expand the settlements. It did not signal a change in underlying Palestinian attitudes, which remain remarkably open to peaceful coexistence with Israelis. Within days of the election, a survey by the Ramallah-based Near East Consulting Institute found that 84 percent of Palestinians in the occupied territories still wanted a negotiated peace, and three-quarters thought Hamas should "change its policy on the elimination of Israel." Even among Hamas supporters, 77 percent said they wanted a negotiated settlement.[7]

After the election, Hamas leaders stated their readiness to end the armed struggle if Israel withdrew to the 1967 lines. Khaled Meshal, the senior leader based in Damascus (who narrowly escaped an Israeli assassination bid in Amman in 1997), wrote in the *Guardian* and the *Los Angeles Times*, "Our message to the Israelis is this: We do not fight you because you belong to a certain faith or culture. Jews have lived in the Muslim world for 13 centuries in peace and harmony; they are in our religion 'the people of the book' who have a covenant from God and His Messenger Muhammad (peace be upon him) to be respected and protected. Our conflict with you is not religious but political."[8] In what was a major step in terms of Hamas's historic position, Meshal told the BBC that his organization would talk to Israel and come to terms, if it "recognises the rights of the Palestinians" and acts "to show and confirm its willingness to withdraw to the 1967 borders."[9] Mousa Abu Marzook, another member of the organization's leadership, hinted that recognition of Israel was a political question, not one of immutable theology: "Where are the borders of the Israel we are supposed to recognize?" he challenged. "Are the settlements included in the borders? Is the return of refugees acceptable to Israel? Until these questions are answered, it is not possible to propose" recognition.[10] In a *Washington Post* op-ed, Abu Marzook also addressed Israelis directly:

> We ask them to reflect on the peace that our peoples once enjoyed and the protection that Muslims gave the Jewish community worldwide. We will exert good-faith efforts to remove the bitterness that Israel's occupation has succeeded in creating, alienating a generation of Palestinians. We call on them not to condemn posterity to endless bloodshed and a conflict in which dominance is illusory. There must come a day when we will live together, side by side once again.[11]

The Hebrew University's Avraham Sela and Tel Aviv University's Shaul Mishal, the two leading Israeli experts on Hamas, observed in their 2000 study, *The Palestinian Hamas: Vision, Violence and Coexistence,* that the organization "is not a prisoner of its own dogmas" and "does not shut itself behind absolute truths, nor does it subordinate its activities and decisions to the officially held religious doctrine." Rather, "Hamas operates in a context of opportunities and constraints, being attentive to the fluctuating needs and desires of the Palestinian population and cognizant of power relations and political feasibility."[12] The two scholars see Hamas as a pragmatic and flexible movement that would be a serious interlocutor willing to figure out a modus vivendi with Israelis. And a surprisingly high 43 percent of Israeli Jews thought that their government should talk to Hamas after the Palestinian election, according to a Tel Aviv University survey.[13]

Yet Hamas is clearly an Islamist movement. Does its rise therefore suggest that Palestinians want to live under an Islamic government? Obviously this would negate the possibility of a single, multireligious state. Until the late 1980s, few Palestinians spoke of the conflict in religious terms. Part of the "Islamicization" of the conflict is a reflection of regional trends, but there are also specific factors. After 1967, Israel emphasized its explicitly religious rationales to justify annexation of East Jerusalem and the establishment of settlements in the occupied territories.[14] This in turn provoked religious counterclaims by Palestinians. Competing exclusivist claims are guaranteed to lead to a totally irreconcilable religious conflict to which there can be no earthly solution. Even Hamas signaled that it understood this, and Abu Marzook wrote in the *Washington Post*, "Our society has always celebrated pluralism in keeping with the unique history and traditions of the Holy Land. In recognizing Judeo-Christian traditions, Muslims nobly vie for and have the greatest incentive and stake in preserving the Holy Land for all three Abrahamic faiths." This is also good, practical politics for a movement that wants to maintain the broadest support; when anonymous leaflets appeared in Gaza threatening to harm churches in retaliation for offensive portrayals of the Prophet Muhammad in European newspapers, Hamas's top leader in Gaza, Mahmoud Zahar, went immediately to visit Gaza's only Catholic church to publicly condemn such threats and express solidarity with Christians.[15]

Yet it is undeniable that there are those among Hamas's leadership and followers who would want to impose Islamic rules on society. This mirrors the growing rise of parallel Jewish movements in Israel, which are contested by the majority of Israelis, who do not want religious theocracy imposed on them. The same debates exist within Palestinian society. Khalil Shikaki, the director of the Palestinian Center for Policy and Survey Research, observed after the election that "survey research during the last decade clearly demonstrates strong public support for liberal democracy among Palestinians." He says, "[M]ost view Israel's democracy more positively than any other in the world, followed by America's."[16] Shikaki pointed out that 55 percent of Palestinians voted for avowedly secular parties. Many Palestinians, Muslim and Christian, are religiously observant and socially conservative, but this in no way translates into backing for a theocracy. Support for an Islamic state among Palestinians has rarely exceeded 3 percent in JMCC polls, and support for an exclusively Palestinian state in all of historic Palestine, without Jews, peaked at 15 percent and usually registers much lower. Adam Hanieh, another Palestinian analyst, dismisses the more lurid fears in the West about the "impending 'Talibanization' of Palestinian society." The vote for Hamas, Hanieh explains, "expressed a political sentiment and desire for a real alternative to the Oslo straitjacket. The Hamas leadership clearly recognizes this and has shown little inclination to implement far-reaching social changes along religious lines."[17] Taking into account the Palestinian population within Israel and the diaspora, where people are generally more secular than in some parts of the occupied territories, no party would be able to impose a single ideology on everyone and would rapidly lose credibility if it did.

Ultimately, it will not be the Hamas leadership but the Palestinian people as a whole who decide these matters, and even under the most oppressive conditions of military occupation, Palestinians have shown that they want to live by democratic and pluralistic rules. Among Palestinians, a single democratic state has been a subject of continued debate. In late 1997, Edward Said, ever a pioneering thinker and iconoclast, challenged prevailing beliefs that the Oslo Accords could still lead to a just and workable Palestinian state. Said wrote that "it has been the failing of Oslo to plan in terms of separation, a clinical partition of peoples into individual, but unequal, entities rather than to grasp that the only way of rising beyond the endless back-and-forth violence and dehumanization is to admit the universality and integrity of the other's experience, and to begin to plan a common life together."[18] Said continued to expand and develop his call for a one-state solution and reconciliation between Israeli Jews and Palestinians up until his untimely death in 2003, and laid the groundwork for other Palestinian thinkers to take up the cause. Azmi Bishara, Joseph Massad, Ghada Karmi, George Bisharat, and Mazin Qumsiyeh are among those who have advocated this approach.[19] The case for a democratic state in all of Israel-Palestine is fairly easy to make among Palestinian exiles and refugees. In most two-state solution proposals, refugees actually lose their rights, so for them the notion of a nationalist Palestinian state within arbitrary borders that do not include the areas they came from is an unattractive prospect.

To many diaspora Palestinians, the whole idea of nationalism as it emerged with post–World War II decolonization has lost its luster, since nation-states in Africa and the Middle East have largely failed to deliver the prosperity and freedom they promised. Those Palestinians working throughout the Middle East have experienced that failure firsthand. Furthermore, the collective experience of diaspora Palestinians in recent decades has been transnational rather than national. We have become used to being Palestinian and Canadian, Palestinian and Colombian, Palestinian and Jordanian—sometimes we hide our identity; other times we boast about it. We have become very good at judging where and how and when to do that, and how to express our identity alongside other identities. Long accustomed to transience and movement, diaspora Palestinians no longer necessarily feel the need for a unidimensional identity embodied by a homogenized, nationalist state. What Palestinians do want and need, though, is freedom of movement and expression, education, and equal access to the benefits of a democratic society. Palestinians want the right to restore their ties with their homeland and its people, and to help build it. Those who believed in a two-state solution for years came to realize that it only offered false promises of peace. There is good reason to believe that, freed from the hardships of occupation, discrimination, and exile, and engaged by Israeli counterparts genuinely interested in building a tolerant, multicultural, multireligious society, the Palestinian majority would gladly, forgivingly, and open-mindedly choose the same course.

Any serious argument for an Israeli-Palestinian democracy in a single state must confront the reality that, at present, Israeli Jews overall are deeply hostile to the idea, viewing it as an invitation to commit suicide. As Israelis come to understand that unilateral solutions based on force provide no remedies to their dilemma, there might be a greater openness to the alternatives that do exist. While this long and difficult process may not happen for years, a handful of Israeli Jews have already begun to think the unthinkable. Meron Benvenisti predicted more than twenty years ago that eventually Israel would be faced with the choice between extremist solutions to maintain its exclusivist "Jewish character," or binationalism. The process, Benvenisti later wrote in 2003, is "apparently inevitable. Israel and the Palestinians are sinking together into the mud of the 'one state.' The question is no longer whether it will be binational, but which model to choose." One of the reasons, Benvenisti argues, that Israelis are so terrified of a binational state is because scaremongers have deliberately equated the idea with the end of Jewish self-determination in Palestine-Israel, rather than a means to achieve it peacefully, and have played up fears that it means being swamped by hostile Arabs. Alternatives exist, Benvenisti points out, that allow Israeli Jews to maintain what they deem essential in a Jewish state, such as a system "that recognizes collective ethnic-national rights and maintains power sharing on the national-central level, with defined political rights for the minority and sometimes territorial-cantonal divisions."[20]

Benvenisti is perhaps far ahead of the curve, but other Israelis are following. Daniel Gavron, for instance, an Israeli journalist and lifelong Zionist, concluded that after the repeated failure of Israelis and Palestinians to agree to a partition, Israelis have taken refuge in what Gavron terms a "solution of despair," which would leave their country a "pathetic ghetto state, cauterized from its neighbors, claustrophobically shut off between the sea and the wall."[21] The "territory between the Mediterranean and the Jordan River must be shared but cannot be sensibly partitioned," Gavron says, so "we are left with only one alternative: Israeli-Palestinian coexistence in one nation."[22] Gavron is acutely aware that most Israelis oppose such a solution because they fear a "nightmare scenario" in which those "with a second passport will depart, and those who don't will be clamoring to get one, fearful it will only be a matter of time until they come under the rule of a not-so-hospitable Arab majority."[23]

The nightmare will only come true, Gavron argues, if Israelis resist inevitable change until they are too weak to prevent it being forced on them. "If we start today," Gavron says, "when we are in charge, it is up to us to create a society in which people want to remain. There is absolutely no reason to believe it would degenerate into something inferior." Gavron continues, "If we create a society in which there are equal rights, democracy, the chance for education and creativity and self-expression, there's absolutely no reason why a very reasonable, enlightened society won't emerge here. I don't see a situation in which suddenly in 20 years, the Arabs have got 61 members of the Knesset, we've only got 59, and then they will turn round and slaughter us in our beds." To me, this is such a hopeful statement and one borne out by precedent, not just in South Africa, but also in the flawed harmony between Israeli Jews and Palestinian citizens within Israel.

In April 2005, at a lecture at Cornell University that included these quotations from Gavron, a prim middle-aged woman, identifying herself as Israeli, accused me of being "completely disconnected from reality." She was convinced that given a chance, Palestinians would kill her and all other Israeli Jews. She urged me to educate myself about the long history of oppression of the Jews and the Holocaust. Her reactions were typical of Israeli Jews when presented with the idea of a joint democratic state.

I acknowledged her fears but asked why it was that in the mixed city of Haifa, Jews were not being murdered by their Arab neighbors. "But they are not Palestinians!" she exclaimed. She genuinely failed to understand that more than one million Arab citizens of Israel are Palestinians distinguished from those in the refugee camps of Lebanon and Gaza only by their experience. Palestinian citizens in Israel often have close relatives in the refugee camps of the region; they often marry Palestinians from the West Bank, Gaza Strip, or Jordan. While Arabs are treated as second-class citizens in Israel, I pointed out they do not murder Jews in their beds. Indignant at my slight against Israeli democracy, the lady responded: "What do you mean? They have rights; they vote in the Knesset!" "Exactly!" I answered. "Give people rights and conflict diminishes." Give them full rights and conflict will in time disappear. I asked her if she knew that Israel's two top soccer heroes in the World Cup qualifying matches were Arabs—Palestinian citizens of Israel. The point was made: When people's rights are recognized, it is possible to stop seeing them as terrorists and murderers and start seeing them as national assets and fellow citizens.

Before us we have two models of Israeli-Palestinian coexistence: one between citizens within Israel, and another between occupier and occupied. It is clear that the first model is the more successful. Palestinian citizens of Israel have lived relatively peacefully with Jews and come to terms with the state *in spite of* the policies and practices devised to deny them equal rights and access to power and opportunities. But their situation is unquestionably better than that of Palestinians in the occupied territories, and would only improve if they had equal rights. Israeli Jews and Palestinians living in mixed cities like Haifa quietly boast of their peaceful, friendly relations; why would we not want to replicate or even improve this model and build on such relative harmony before it is lost as Israel continues to institute racist policies in an attempt to consolidate its "Jewish character"? While the fearful Israeli woman's concerns are nothing new, her ignorance of the situation of Israel's Palestinian citizens was astounding. "So am I crazy?" I asked a young Israeli man from Haifa who came over at the end of the lecture. "You are not crazy at all, but you see the difficulty we face in Israel," he said, alluding to the woman who had spoken out. "There is a big difference between the younger and older generations, and things will change."

Israeli Jews were not always so terrified of the Palestinians whom they rule in the occupied territories. Gavron recalls how in the two decades after the 1967 war and before the first Intifada, for Israelis, "traveling through ... the West Bank became routine. From Jerusalem we would drive north to Galilee or south to the Negev desert without thinking twice about it. We would vacation on the beautiful Sinai coast, hike through the Golan Heights, and enjoy meals in the charming outdoor restaurants of Bethlehem and Jericho."[24] My relatives in Battir remember many such visitors, drawn by the village's lush terraces planted with every variety of fruit, and Saturday shopping in the West Bank town of Tulkarm was a regular event for Israelis from the nearby coastal region. Palestinian tolerance during this period points to the fallacy of the claim that many in Israel and America continue to make: that Palestinians are inherently hostile to Israelis and would murder them at any opportunity. Today, few Israelis would dare to venture into the heart of a Palestinian city, unless they were riding in a tank or a bulldozer, but it took decades to reach today's level of hostility.

While Israelis shopped and ate in Palestinian towns and seized Palestinian lands, Palestinians themselves traveled freely to every part of the country to take up the jobs that Israelis once did themselves—construction work, picking fruit, and cleaning.

Palestinians and Israelis sometimes formed intimate and mutually dependent relationships. Danae Elon, the daughter of Amos Elon, a vocal Israeli critic of the occupation, explored the relationship between her family and that of their Palestinian servant from the West Bank in her highly acclaimed 2004 film *Another Road Home*. Musa Obeidallah from Battir worked for the family for eighteen hours a day from the time Danae was born until she grew up. Musa faithfully ironed her uniform when she went to do her military service in the army of occupation. Through making the film, Danae learns what this relationship truly meant to Musa and his family. First, she discovers that "Musa" is not even his real name, but one he adopted to spare Israelis the difficulty of having to pronounce "Mahmoud," which includes a guttural "h" sound that Ashkenazi Hebrew speakers find difficult to make. She also learns how Musa's children, now owners of a pharmacy in the gritty industrial town of Paterson, New Jersey, grew up without their father as he devoted their childhoods to caring for the Elons so he could earn enough to send them to university. She learns how Musa's children knew so much about her life yet she was oblivious to theirs. Danae only truly gets to know Musa once they meet outside the context of military occupation and the inescapable imbalance of power that makes equal human relations impossible. Another powerful document is the 1989 book *My Enemy, My Self* by Israeli journalist Yoram Binur, who spent almost a year undercover disguised as a Palestinian day laborer. Binur recounts his experience along with Palestinians from across the occupied territories vying for ill-paid and backbreaking day work at Tel Aviv's "slave market." Together with Palestinians from Gaza's Rafah refugee camp, he slept in illegal, rat-infested boardinghouses in Tel Aviv kept by Jewish employers to help the workers evade the tough regulations prohibiting overnight stays.[25] Hundreds of thousands of workers like Musa and those encountered by Binur, some of them my own family from Battir, worked in Israel for years, forming the invisible underclass on which the Israeli economy came to rely. But Palestinians also learned Hebrew and came to terms with the irrevocable reality of the Israeli presence. This coexistence of sorts ended with the outbreak of the first Intifada in 1987, which signaled that Palestinians had had enough. Today Danae Elon says that the account of Palestine-Israel she gave in her film "is not two separate stories but one," because "the two people[s] are completely interrelated and intertwined on every possible level," and "in reality, Palestine is Israel today and Israel is Palestine." She is one of the new generation of Israelis who dares to say that "the only solution that is viable" is a single state for both peoples.[26]

Even when Israeli Jews once more come to understand that Palestinians are not bloodthirsty murderers, there remains the argument that Israel is needed as a Jewish safe haven. One Israeli peace activist friend presented the prevailing Zionist view when she reported the comments of her mother, a refugee who fled Germany in 1935: "'The state of Israel makes sure that next time we will not die unprotected, but with a rifle in our hand'; for this reason, Jews cannot afford the luxury of understanding the Palestinian point of view." Such views, my friend was suggesting, are so deeply entrenched that there is simply no point challenging them. But one could argue that the most dangerous place in the world to be a Jew is in Israel-Palestine, and that this is the direct result of the conflict that arose from establishing a state that benefits and privileges Jews in a country already populated by a non-Jewish majority. The point is not to deny Jews a safe haven in Palestine-Israel, but to make the necessary changes that can at last allow it to become one for the first time since Israel was founded.

There is some evidence that other Israeli Jews are open to imagining a joint future. One such person is Aron Trauring, the creator of the Web site Aron's Israel Peace Weblog. Trauring's mother and her family fled Belgium after the Nazi invasion, eventually ending up in America; Aron Trauring himself was born into an observant Orthodox Jewish family in New York in 1954 and eventually moved to Israel, where he and his wife raised four children. At the height of the second Intifada, Trauring's third son decided to become a conscientious objector. "The army really lashes out at these young people," Aron explains, and "at this point I said I've had enough and if people want to be suicidal, that's their choice, but it's something I am going to opt out of." In 2002, after twenty years in Israel, Trauring and his wife returned to the United States. Aron's questioning of Israel's policies began during his military service in the first Intifada, when he witnessed severe abuse of Palestinians by the army. After he returned to civilian life, it gnawed at him. "One of the things we grew up on is that the world was silent while the Jews were being killed," he recalls, "so you have this value that 'you will stand up against injustice.' And inside I am saying to myself, 'you didn't stand up against injustice, you didn't raise your hand to stop it, you participated in it.'"[27]

Trauring's approach now is pragmatic and humanistic: "We

have to say whatever the past, whatever the origins of the conflict, you have several million Jews living there and several
million Arabs and both of these people feel this is their home,
like my children. You can't say this was once the Palestinian
home, so all the Jews should go back. On the other hand, why
is it okay for my children to live in Israel, while the children of
Palestinian refugees can't come back? How can that be just to
say we'll have this thing where they'll be over there and we'll
be over here. It isn't just." As much as he grappled with the
dilemma, Trauring could not see how to partition the country
without perpetuating existing injustices or creating new ones
that would only spur more conflict.

For Trauring, the only way out of the dead end is to change
the terms of the discussion. "As long as we are talking about the
right to land, [the discussion] is threatening to both peoples," he
explains. "Who cares who owns the land? Everyone who lives
there owns the land. The issue is how can all the people who live
there have equal rights. How can all the people live under the
principles of the Universal Declaration of Human Rights?" If
people accept the principle of democracy, Aron explains, then
the whole need for separate ethnic states for Israelis and Palestinians falls away and solves the problem of who lives where.
"What does garbage collection have to do with being Jewish?"
he asks. "What does it have to do with being Arab? How you
run a police force, all the functions of a state, what does that
have to do with your ethnicity?" Where culture does matter is
with respect to issues like education, but here Aron points out
the contradictions that already exist in Jewish Israel. For
instance, there are three school systems, one for secular Jewish

students, one for Orthodox Jews, and another for the ultra-Orthodox. "So even in this Jewish state," Trauring argues, "you have three school systems, so why can't you have different cultural education in a multiethnic state?" Despite pessimism about the current state of affairs, Trauring retains an abiding faith that "except for the settlers, who say God gave us this land and democracy is worthless, the vast majority of Israelis are not going to say no, we are not going to be a democracy." The conversation about civil rights and democracy, rather than sovereignty over land, Trauring is convinced, "will be a lot more disturbing to Israelis," but ultimately, he believes, they "have a strong commitment to social justice and democracy, and . . . confronting them with these contradictions between their values and what they are doing" will provide a way forward.

Trauring is almost certainly right that the most zealous settlers could never come to terms with coexisting with the Palestinians. That may not matter should the majority of Israelis ever opt for a multiethnic democracy. But at least one sympathizer with the religious settler movement proved that even in that community conversions are not impossible. David Landau also moved to Israel from the United States after high school, becoming Orthodox and joining the Israeli army as part of a Hesder yeshiva combat unit made up of religious students who study and serve together. He served in the army's elite Givati Brigade and became a vigorous supporter of the Gush Emunim religious settler movement. He admired the settlers as if they were pioneers taming the Wild West. But, as for Trauring, the experience of policing the occupation during the first

Intifada plunged him into a lengthy period of introspection. "I was really, really torn because there was a part of me that saw the occupation as horrible and yet there was a part of me that saw a need for the occupation, or the belief that it was justified somehow," Landau remembers. "And so I feel a little sort of like the South African who lives under apartheid" and "somehow justifies the apartheid."[28]

Landau reached the same conclusion shared by Ehud Olmert and the majority of Israeli Jews who support unilateral separation: Israel could not continue to rule the Palestinians forever. But his thinking led him in a very different direction: "A Jewish state that occupies people and keeps them down didn't make sense anymore and if that's what it was going to take to have a Jewish state, then it didn't deserve to be a Jewish state." Ultimately, Landau predicts that Israelis will understand that their country cannot be "exclusively Jewish," and he hopes to see it transformed into "a democratic state that supports all members of its population, respects them and treats them well." He hopes that Israel will turn from being an isolated garrison into a "crossroads of cultures" and a "center of commerce, trade, conversation and negotiation." After several tours of duty in the occupied territories, Landau decided to return to the United States. But he dreams of going back to Israel. "I've been very homesick. . . . There's such a vibrancy in the life there," he says wistfully. "There's a part of my soul that talks to me there."

Within Israel there are expressions of similar sentiments, however tentative. In June 2004, a group of Israeli Jewish intellectuals gathered at the beach resort of Giv'at Olga and issued an extraordinary statement, which read in part:

We are united in the recognition that this country belongs to all its sons and daughters—citizens and residents, both present and absentees (the uprooted Palestinian citizens of Israel in '48)—with no discrimination on personal or communal grounds, irrespective of citizenship or nationality, religion, culture, ethnicity or gender. Thus we demand the immediate annulment of all laws, regulations and practices that discriminate between Jewish and Arab citizens of Israel, and the dissolution of all institutions, organizations and authorities based on such laws, regulations and practices.[29]

Signed by over one hundred Israeli Jews, many of them prominent academics, the "Olga Document" leaves open the form of coexistence, whether it be in one or two states, or some kind of federation, but as its signatories affirm, only the principles of equality and taking responsibility for Israel's actions can "lay the foundations on which the people of this country can set up the proper common frameworks for life together." The Olga Document challenges Israelis "to take the first step in the long journey that can extricate [them] from the tangle of denial, repression, distortion of reality, loss of direction, and forsaking of conscience in which the people of Israel have been trapped for generations." As far-reaching as the document is, in Israeli terms, the immediate goal of its authors is modest: "We seek to start off a genuine public discussion about the Israeli blind alley in which we live and the profound changes needed in order to break out of it." That is exactly what needs to happen now, not only among Israeli Jews but among Palestinians and all who desire peace.

*   *   *

With the failure of the two-state solution and ongoing realignments within both Israeli and Palestinian politics, we are at a moment of profound uncertainty and risk but also of tantalizing opportunity. There is no credible "peace process" to provide hope that the misery on the ground is merely a transitory phase on the way to deliverance, and the one big idea that is supposed to save us—the Palestinian state—lies in tatters. There is a need for urgent action on two fronts: One is in the realm of dialogue, imagination, and construction of an inclusive vision. At the same time, there is a pressing need for resistance to the outcome Israel is trying to impose on the Palestinians, one that can only lead to greater bloodshed and suffering on all sides. These appear to be contradictory mandates, but they must go hand in hand.

In South Africa, the ANC was able to put forward a vision that eventually convinced most whites that their best interests lay in participation rather than rejection. If those who support Palestinian rights fail to dedicate themselves to constructing such a vision, Israelis who desire change will find their backs pressed further up against an intransigent wall, leading to even more extreme measures than the prison regime of settlements and checkpoints. Benny Elon, the leading advocate of forced "transfer" for all Palestinians, knows that he does not have majority support now. He is patiently laying the groundwork for the day when Israelis see no other way to ensure their own survival. Those voices in Israel calling for selective non-Jewish birth control and other abhorrent measures will only gain strength as partition fails and leaves a vacuum. Palestinians, too, robbed of hope, will gravitate to ever more radical and extreme approaches. It is vital to show both peoples that there is another way: we must insist on a debate over alternatives to the two-state solution that will allow each community to secure its rights, identity, and legitimacy by embracing the other as equal. The debate I propose is not an idle intellectual exercise: By talking of a common future and imagining it, we engage in the act of creating it; we introduce a different prospect to endless war. It is only through shattering taboos, questioning long-held assumptions, and articulating a vision that we can move the idea of coexistence in a single state from the far margins to the center of discussion. Simply by admitting the notion to the range of possibilities, we change the landscape.

At the same time, without resistance to raise the cost of the status quo, few Israeli Jews will have much incentive to question their government's policy and force a change of direction. It is human to hold on even to a dismal present for fear of a more uncertain future. We must, therefore, push forward with an international struggle to resist and dismantle Israel's inhumane policies, which are implemented with complicity from the United States, Europe, and some Arab governments. Every Palestinian is in a position to demand that the leadership engage in a struggle that is not only morally defensible but effective, one that mobilizes the greatest number of people in civil disobedience and mass demonstrations that make the system of walls, checkpoints, land confiscations, and new settlements ungovernable and unworkable. This can only work when combined with an international campaign to isolate Israel for as long as it pursues these measures. Within Palestine-Israel, more than 170 Palestinian organizations, unions, and institutions have supported the Palestinian Campaign for the Academic and Cultural Boycott of Israel, which stresses that it targets Israeli institutions that refuse to condemn and work against the occupation and other discriminatory state policies. The campaign calls on people worldwide to follow suit. In February 2006, dozens of prominent Israeli filmmakers and artists signed a statement recognizing the main premise for this boycott—that there can be no normal relations between Palestinian and Israeli institutions that do not oppose the occupation, while occupation and radical inequality persist.[30] At every stage, it must be made clear that the campaign is not aimed at Israelis as human beings but at the unjust system their government has built. There can be no place in this struggle for violence that targets Israeli civilians.

Palestinians and their allies already have assets to build on, though it is important to realize that their struggle is significantly different from that against South African apartheid in a number of ways. The apartheid regime enjoyed strong support from the United States as an ally in the battle against what Washington saw as revolutionary communism spreading in southern Africa. Many U.S. and European corporations were heavily invested in South Africa's industries, especially its mines. The Reagan administration and the government of Margaret Thatcher both strongly resisted the imposition of sanctions until they were forced to succumb to enormous public and international pressure. Within the United States and the United Kingdom, the South African government had staunch allies on the political right. Chester Crocker, Reagan's envoy to Southern Africa and architect of the policy of "constructive engagement" toward Pretoria, told a South African reporter, "All Reagan knows about South Africa is that he's on the side of the whites."[31] Many right-wing think tanks that were perhaps less ignorant also sided with Pretoria. The American evangelical leader Jerry Falwell, a Christian Zionist supporter of Israel today, was a prominent apologist for the apartheid regime in the early 1980s. But beyond these albeit influential circles, there was no broad ideological constituency of support for Afrikaner nationalism per se, comparable to the pro-Israel Zionist constituencies in the United States. Moreover, the fall of the Berlin Wall in November 1989 and the end of the Soviet era certainly diminished the U.S.–South African alliance and hastened the collapse of apartheid. By contrast, in the global war of the early twenty-first century, "the war against terror," Israel is seen as a key U.S. ally in the struggle against an amorphous Islamic extremism of which the Palestinians are alleged to be an element. Groups like Hamas, which to Palestinians are part of a legitimate national resistance, are viewed by Washington as enemies.

In another difference, the United States Congress, under the leadership of the Congressional Black Caucus, was key in forcing the Reagan administration to abandon "constructive engagement" and eventually impose sanctions on South Africa. The antiapartheid movement struck deep chords in America, where the civil rights struggle was so recent, and supporting sanctions became in effect a test of a politician's commitment to civil rights at home as much as a foreign-policy position. In the case of Israel-Palestine, Congress stands as one of the leading obstacles to a sensible Middle East policy, consistently passing resolutions endorsing by huge margins virtually any position placed before it by AIPAC lobbyists (the handful of representatives who have voted most consistently against such resolutions have also often been members of the Congressional Black Caucus).

Thus Palestinians face an even greater struggle for support than did apartheid's opponents. Still, apartheid nonetheless had powerful allies who helped Pretoria resist change until the end. Ultimately, governments and businesses with investments in South Africa only started to divest when broad-based public campaigns rendered such dealings morally unacceptable and politically untenable. And despite efforts by the American and Israeli right wings, on the one hand, and some Islamist ideologues on the other, to portray the Palestinian struggle as part of a generalized war of civilizations between Islam and the West, it remains widely accepted that the conflict is one of a struggle for power between two peoples in a specific piece of land and that it requires a political solution.

One common misconception about the antiapartheid struggle is that the ANC masterminded the global campaign of sanctions and boycotts that eventually made white South Africans understand they needed to change. The reality is that while the ANC and other parties directed the struggle within the country, its real contribution to the global campaign was not organizational but visionary. Much of the activism was simply ad hoc. As for the PLO, its older leadership never much appreciated the importance of building an international movement. Its strategy was always focused on winning diplomatic recognition from world leaders. The PLO and later the Palestinian Authority were obsessed with behaving like a government, setting up "embassies" in prestigious capitals when they should have been leading a liberation campaign. Time and again, Palestinian leaders have been confronted with the reality that just sitting at a table with James Baker or Bill Clinton does not constitute influence.

Yet despite a crippling lack of coherence and vision from their leadership, Palestinians have neither weakened nor faded away as Israeli leaders hoped and predicted. Both the steadfastness of Palestinians on the ground, who have refused to abandon their claim to rights and dignity, and the support of the Palestinian diaspora have helped hold the line against the assault on the validity of their cause. In small towns and college campuses all across America there is always a dedicated, savvy, and fearless local group with perhaps five, ten, or twenty members challenging the local Zionist establishment. Even more striking is that several newer Palestinian rights groups do not include a single Palestinian—a confirmation that the struggle has enormous universal appeal.

This movement is growing. Student groups have forced the issue of Palestinian rights and U.S. support for Israeli abuses into the mainstream; they have put forward resolutions calling on universities to divest pension funds and other assets from companies whose work profits from or supports the Israeli occupation. Campaigns that started on university campuses have already moved into the larger society. In July 2004, the General Assembly of the Presbyterian Chuch USA passed a resolution calling for selective divestment from companies whose work in Israel contributes to the oppression of Palestinians. The immediate effect of this resolution was to spark vigorous debate in Presbyterian congregations across the country. The leading national pro-Israel organizations mobilized all their resources to try to halt the momentum, but in 2005 the United Church of Christ followed the Presbyterian lead.

In February 2006, the Church of England voted, with the support of its global leader, the Archbishop of Canterbury, to divest from all "companies profiting from the illegal occupation" of Palestinian territories.[32] Consequently efforts were made to force the church to sell several million dollars' worth of stock in Caterpillar, the U.S. company whose bulldozers are routinely used to demolish Palestinian homes. The same month a group of sixty architects, including some of the most prominent British practitioners, met to consider a boycott targeting the Israeli construction industry because in their view, "planning, architecture and other construction disciplines are being used to promote an apartheid system of environmental control." The fact that such boycotts are not anti-Israeli but pro-justice was highlighted by Eyal Weizman, the Israeli director of the architecture center at London's prestigious Goldsmith College, who concurred that because the wall and the settlements were deemed illegal by the International Court of Justice, "[W]e should boycott any company which does business, any architects that participate—anyone facilitating these human rights violations and war crimes."[33] Then, in May 2006, the convention of the 200,000-strong Ontario branch of the Canadian Union of Public Employees voted overwhelmingly to support the international campaign of boycott, divestment, and sanctions as long as Israel maintained its current policies, as did the UK's largest university lecturers union, the National Association of Teachers in Further and Higher Education.[34]

These campaigns have faced fierce resistance. But they have put many pro-Israeli government groups on the defensive and have exposed Israeli and U.S. government policies to the close scrutiny from which they had always been shielded. The ADL has been so alarmed by the upsurge in activism that it has worked hard to scare people away from involvement by waving the banner of anti-Semitism. ADL director Abraham Foxman published an article setting out what he called "litmus tests to assess when criticism of Israel crosses the line" into anti-Semitism. In a remarkably intolerant passage, he wrote: "First, let me say anti-Zionism is anti-Semitism. There should be no debate about that."[35] The associate dean of the Simon Wiesenthal Center, Rabbi Abraham Cooper, set a new standard in moral blackmail by labeling a United Church of Christ resolution calling on Israel to dismantle the illegal West Bank separation wall "functionally anti-Semitic."[36]

The ferocity of these reactions demonstrate that the growing divestment movement is a powerfully effective tool. True, counterpressure has sometimes succeeded in stifling debate. In January 2006, for example, after a government minister in Norway supported a regional Norwegian decision to impose a boycott on Israeli goods, she was forced to retract her position; Norway's foreign minister apologized to Israel and the United States, promising that "it has never been and will never be the position of the Norwegian government to advocate any such policy toward Israel."[37] Weeks later, the American Association of University Professors, under pressure from pro-Israel groups including the ADL, canceled a conference in which pro-boycott professors were due to participate.[38] The intensity of these efforts perhaps indicates the Israeli establishment's realization that it is on shaky and ultimately indefensible grounds. A confidential ten-year forecast produced in 2004 by Israel's foreign ministry concluded that the country is on a collision course with Europe and could be isolated as a pariah state, like apartheid South Africa, if the conflict is not resolved soon.[39] The contradictions that made this assessment valid in 2004 have only increased.

Since decades of worldwide protest have not succeeded in bringing about a Palestinian state or weakening Israel's hold on the occupied territories, one might argue that such protest can hardly be expected to bring about a joint democratic state. Though compelling, this objection misses the point. Palestinians do not have the political or material strength to stop the settlements and walls that have rendered a two-state solution unworkable. But Israel's might is useless in a struggle that is not about winning territory but securing democratic rights for all. This is why opposition to the grim realities must be coupled with a battle of ideas in which walls and checkpoints provide no defense. Furthermore, it is why the struggle must take a moral form that offers Israel no excuses for its oppressive measures.

The global campaign for Palestinian rights and against Israeli injustice, despite the counterattack, continues to grow, through ad hoc grassroots alliances between Palestinian activists and civil society and their allies around the world, including some in Israel.[40] The campaigns copy the tactics of the antiapartheid struggle, but there is a lack of strategic coherence, which is related to the absence of a unifying vision. Even those who are convinced that a one-state solution offers the only possibility for peace and justice are reluctant to call for it openly. At the moment, there is not enough consensus around it, thus the urgent task is to build such a consensus.

The *New York Times* columnist Thomas Friedman visited the West Bank in 2003 and saw the wall that Israel had built completely encircling the city of Qalqilya, part of the larger separation wall system. Friedman concluded that "[r]ather than create the outlines of a two-state solution, this wall will kill that idea for Palestinians, and drive them, over time, to demand instead a one-state solution—where they and the Jews would have equal rights. . . ." Friedman warned that "this transformation of the Palestinian cause will be very problematic for Israel. If American Jews think it's hard to defend Israel today on college campuses, imagine what it will be like when their kids have to argue against the principle of one man, one vote."[41] Friedman exhorted Israel to rush to create a truncated Palestinian state along the lines of the Camp David proposals to save itself from this fate. But since he wrote those words, the wall has continued to snake its way through the West Bank, as new settlements—some now populated by settlers who evacuated Gaza—proliferate.

Friedman's alarm should be taken as implicit recognition that Israel's insistence on maintaining its exclusivist Jewish character, in spite of the reality that Palestine-Israel is and has always been a multicultural, multireligious country, is a chauvinistic appeal to ethnic tribalism that stands no chance in a contest against democratic and universal principles. Although he may be appalled by this, I can't help but find Friedman's discomfiture most encouraging. This is one of those moments when ordinary people can, through talking, acting, thinking, and imagining together, improve the lives of millions of Israelis and Palestinians. Perhaps, by transforming the country from a place of misery and death to a normal society, those same ordinary people can truly change the world for the better.

NOTES

INTRODUCTION

1. For a brief history of Lifta, see Walid Khalidi, *All That Remains: The Palestinian Villages Occupied and Depopulated by Israel in 1948* (Washington, DC: Institute for Palestine Studies, 1992), pp. 300–303.
2. Cited in ibid., p. 301.
3. Benny Morris, *The Birth of the Palestinian Refugee Problem, 1947–1949* (Cambridge, UK: Cambridge University Press, 1987), p. 50.
4. Ibid., p. 52.
5. Tom Segev, *One Palestine, Complete: Jews and Arabs under the British Mandate* (New York: Metropolitan Books, 2000), pp. 325–26.
6. See, for example, Alan Sipress, "Hebron descendants decry actions of current settlers. They are kin of the Jews ousted in 1929," The Philadelphia Inquirer, 3 March 1997.
7. See chapter 3 for a full discussion of such extremist approaches.

1: AN IMPOSSIBLE PARTITION

1. Hansard, Oral Debates, November 29, 2005, Column 115.
2. See *Report of the Palestine Royal Commission, Summary of the Report* (London: United Kingdom Government, 1937). Available online from UNISPAL (United Nations Information System on the Question of Palestine), http://domino.un.org/unispal.nsf.
3. United Nations Special Commission on Palestine (UNSCOP), *Report to the General Assembly,* vol. 1. (Lake Success, NY: 1947), UN Document A/364. September 3, 1947, p. 39.

4. Avi Shlaim, *The Iron Wall* (New York: Norton, 2000), p. 25.

5. UNSCOP, *Report to the General Assembly*, vol. 3, annex A (Lake Success, NY: 1947), UN Document A/364 Add. 2. September 3, 1947, pp. 92–93.

6. UNSCOP, *Report to the General Assembly*, vol. 6, annex B (Lake Success, NY: 1947), UN Document A/364 Add. 3. September 3, 1947, pp. 42–43.

7. See Sami Hadawi, *Village Statistics* (Beirut: Palestine Liberation Organization Research Center, 1970). Hadawi had been an official land valuer and inspector of tax assessments in the Palestine government. This book is an annotated reproduction of the data put out by the Mandate government in its latter years under the same title.

8. UNSCOP, *Report to the General Assembly*, vol. 1, p. 48.

9. Ibid., p. 54.

10. Ibid., p. 47.

11. Foundation for Middle East Peace, "Israeli settlements in the occupied territories: a guide; a special report of the Foundation for Middle East Peace," March 2002, http://www.fmep.org.

12. "Judea" and "Samaria," biblical terms for regions roughly congruent with the West Bank, are routinely used by the Israeli state and the mainstream Zionist movement to convey a territorial claim and historical presence.

13. United Nations, "Report of the Special Committee to investigate Israeli practices affecting the human rights of the population of the Occupied Territories," November 13, 1979, Document A/34/631.

14. Mattiyahu Drobles, "Master plan for the Development of Settlement in Judea and Samaria" (1980), cited in Ibrahim Matar, "Exploitation of Land and Water Resources for Jewish Colonies in the Occupied Territories," in *International Law and the Administration of Occupied Territories*, ed. Emma Playfair (Oxford, UK: Oxford University Press, 1992), p. 443, cited in Ardi Imseis, "On the Fourth Geneva Convention and the Occupied Palestinian Territory," *Harvard International Law Journal* 44, no. 1 (2003), p. 104.

15. Foundation for Middle East Peace, "Table: Israeli Settler Population in the West Bank, 1972–2004," http://www.fmep.org.

16. *Statistical Yearbook of Jerusalem,* 2003, Table III/13; Table X/12, cited by Foundation for Middle East Peace, http://www.fmep.org.

17. Nadav Shagrai, "B'Tselem report: settlers control 41.9% of West Bank," *Ha'aretz,* May 13, 2002, http://www.haaretzdaily.com.

18. Amir Cheshin, Bill Hutman, and Avi Melamed, *Separate and Unequal: The Inside Story of Israeli Rule in East Jerusalem* (Cambridge, MA: Harvard University Press, 1999), pp. 32–33.

19. Ibid., p. 10.

20. Ibid., pp. 50–53.

21. Christine Hauser, "Palestinians feel like underdogs against King David," *New York Times,* July 9, 2005.

22. "Planning and building: statistics on demolition of houses built without permits," http://www.btselem.org (undated).

23. Ghassan Khatib, "Behind the Smokescreen," *Bitter Lemons,* June 13, 2005, available at http://www.bitterlemons.org/previous/bl300613ed20.html#pal1 (accessed September 22, 2005).

24. "Israel gears up for new settlement masterplan," *Agence France Presse,* September 1, 2005.

25. Amira Hass, lecture, Barnard College, April 11, 2005.

26. "West Bank closure count and analysis," UN Office for the Coordination of Humanitarian Affairs, January 2006, http://www.humanitarianinfo.org/opt/docs/UN/OCHA/OCHAoPt_ClosureAnalysis0106_En.pdf.

27. Rima Merriman, "The making of an Israeli factoid," *The Electronic Intifada,* May 5, 2005, http://electronicintifada.net/v2/article3820.shtml.

28. "Report of the Special Rapporteur of the Commission on Human Rights on the situation of human rights in the Palestinian territories occupied by Israel since 1967," August 12, 2004, UN General Assembly Document A/59/256.

29. Aluf Benn, "Quietly carrying on building," *Ha'aretz,* January 8, 2005.

30. "Legal consequences of the construction of a wall in the Occupied Palestinian Territory," advisory opinion of the International Court of Justice, July 9, 2004, available at http://www.icj-cij.org.

31. Jeff Halper, "Beyond Road Maps & Walls," *The Link* 37, no. 1 (January–March 2004).

32. Patrick Wintour, "Alarm at US drift over Middle East," *Guardian*, July 21, 2004.

33. Aaron Miller, "Israel's Lawyer," *Washington Post*, May 23, 2005.

34. J. Boudreault et al., *U.S. Official Statements: Israeli Settlements; the Fourth Geneva Convention* (Washington, DC: Institute for Palestine Studies, 1992), p. 3.

35. Interview with Robert Siegel on National Public Radio's *All Things Considered*, June 24, 2004. Transcript available at http://www.npr.org/programs/atc/transcripts/2002/jun/020624.siegel2.html.

36. Letter from President George W. Bush to Prime Minister Ariel Sharon, dated April 14, 2004, available at http://www.whitehouse.gov.

37. Speech by President Clinton at Israel Policy Dinner, January 7, 2001. Transcript available at http://www.clintonfoundation.org/legacy/01071-speech-by-president-at-israel-policy-dinner.htm (accessed March 7, 2006).

38. Laurie Copans, "Pat Robertson warns Bush against dividing Jerusalem," Associated Press, October 4, 2004.

39. John Chase, "Obama, Keyes, clash on terrorism; Senate hopefuls clarify stances," *Chicago Tribune*, October 11, 2004.

40. Tom Hundley, "Sharon moves more; life out of jeopardy," *Chicago Tribune*, January 11, 2006.

41. "Unrwa Completes Its Demolition Assessment of Operation Rainbow," press release, UNRWA, Gaza City, May 26, 2004 (Ref. HQ/G/16/2004).

42. "Investigation of the IDF Action in Rafah," B'Tselem press release, May 15, 2004.

43. Press conference at United Nations Headquarters, New York, June 25, 2004.

44. Ghada Karmi, "With no Palestinian state in sight, aid becomes an adjunct to occupation," *Guardian*, December 31, 2006.

45. Chris McGreal, "Hamas leader accuses West of hypocrisy over threat to withhold cash," *Guardian*, March 8, 2006.

46. Israeli author Yitzhak Laor noted that "a report published on 6 September [2002] in the (right-wing) daily *Ma'ariv* revealed that during the first three weeks of the [second] Intifada—before the wave of terror attacks against Israelis even began—the IDF [Israeli Defense Forces], according to Army records, fired one million bullets" (Yitzhak Laor, "Diary," *London Review of Books*, October 3, 2002). Laor later elaborated, citing an article in *Ha'aretz* from June 11, 2004: "A month after the Intifada began, four years ago, Major General Amos Malka, by then No. 3 in the military hierarchy, and until 2001 the head of Israeli military Intelligence (MI), asked one of his officers (Major Kuperwasser) how many 5.56 mm bullets the Central Command had fired during that month (that is, only in the West Bank). Three years later Malka talked about these horrific figures. This is what he said to *Ha'aretz*'s diplomatic commentator Akiva Eldar about the first month of the Intifada, 30 days of unrest, no terrorist attacks yet, no Palestinian shooting: 'Kuperwasser got back to me with the number, 850,000 bullets. My figure was 1.3 million bullets in the West Bank and Gaza. This is a strategic figure that says that our soldiers are shooting and shooting and shooting. I asked: "Is this what you intended in your preparations?" and he replied in the negative. I said: "Then the significance is that we are determining the height of the flames." ' " (Yitzhak Laor, "A bullet fired for every Palestinian child," *Counterpunch*, October 21, 2004). It is also worth noting that the high-profile investigative committee headed by former U.S. senator George Mitchell stated in its final report: "The GOI [Government of Israel] asserts that the immediate catalyst for the violence was the breakdown of the Camp David negotiations on July 25, 2000 and the 'widespread appreciation in the international community of Palestinian responsibility for the impasse.' In this view, Palestinian violence was planned by the PA [Palestinian Authority] leadership, and was aimed at 'provoking and incurring Palestinian casualties as a means of regaining the diplomatic initiative.' " The report continued: "In their submissions, the parties traded allegations about the motivation and degree of control exercised by the other. However, we were provided with no persuasive evidence that the Sharon visit was anything other

than an internal political act; neither were we provided with persuasive evidence that the PA planned the uprising." The report added that, "[a]ccordingly, we have no basis on which to conclude that there was a deliberate plan by the PA to initiate a campaign of violence at the first opportunity; or to conclude that there was a deliberate plan by the GOI to respond with lethal force." Finally, the Mitchell commission concluded: "The Sharon visit did not cause the 'Al-Aqsa Intifada.' But it was poorly timed and the provocative effect should have been foreseen; indeed it was foreseen by those who urged that the visit be prohibited. More significant were the events that followed: the decision of the Israeli police on September 29 [2000] to use lethal means against the Palestinian demonstrators; and the subsequent failure, as noted above, of either party to exercise restraint" (see "Sharm El-Sheikh Fact-Finding Committee Report," April 30, 2001, available at http://www.state.gov/p/nea/rls/rpt/3060.htm [accessed March 10, 2006]).

47. *Ruling Palestine: A History of the Legally Sanctioned Jewish-Israeli Seizure of Land and Housing in Palestine* (Geneva: Centre on Housing Rights and Eviction, in collaboration with BADIL Resource Center for Palestinian Residency and Refugee Rights, May 2005).

48. Yoel Esteron, "Needed: a great soul," *Ha'aretz*, August 30, 2004.

49. Gideon Levy, "Civics lesson at Kfar Maimon," *Ha'aretz*, July 24, 2005.

50. Yoav Stern, "Poll: Most Israeli Jews say Israeli Arabs should emigrate," *Ha'aretz*, April 4, 2005.

51. Amira Hass, lecture, Barnard College, April 11, 2005.

52. Jerusalem Media and Communications Centre, "JMCC Public Opinion Poll No. 37 on Palestinian Attitudes Towards Final Status Negotiations and the declaration of the State—June 2000," available at http://www.jmcc.org/publicpoll/results/2000/no37.htm.

2: "THE STATE OF ISRAEL IS COMING TO AN END"

1. Ori Nir, "Demographics drive Likud's shifting agenda," *Forward*, December 26, 2003.

2. Gershom Gorenberg, "A birthday for my teenager, a decision for Israel," *Washington Post*, December 14, 2003.

3. Larry Derfner, "Sounding the alarm about Israel's demographic crisis," *Forward*, January 9, 2004.

4. Amiram Barakat, "For first time, Jews no longer a majority in pre-pullout Israel," *Ha'aretz*, August 12, 2005.

5. Paul Holmes, "Israel's 'Arab counter' influences land debate," Reuters, January 12, 2006.

6. Yigal Allon, "The case for defensible borders," *Foreign Affairs* (October 1976).

7. Graham Usher, "Bantustanisation or Bi-Nationalism? An Interview with Azmi Bishara," *Race & Class* 37, no. 2 (October 1995).

8. Joel Brinkley, "Israeli Labor Party opens campaign; asks halt in rule over Arabs," *New York Times*, September 6, 1988.

9. Asher Wallfish, "Rabin is the bearer of Allon's mantle," *Jerusalem Post*, November 11, 1988.

10. Clyde Haberman, "Shamir is said to admit to plan to stall talks 'for 10 years,'" *New York Times*, June 27, 1992.

11. Connie Bruck, "The Wounds of Peace," *New Yorker*, October 14, 1996, pp. 64–91.

12. Ibid., p. 66.

13. Ibid., p. 70.

14. Ibid., p. 72.

15. Interview on *Democracy Now!*, February 5, 2006.

16. Bruck, p. 75.

17. Daniel Gavron, *The Other Side of Despair: Jews and Arabs in the Promised Land* (Lanham, MD: Rowman and Littlefield, 2004), p. 154.

18. Ibid., p. 161.

19. CNN Late Edition with Wolf Blitzer, November 11, 2001, transcript no. 111100CN.V47.

20. Thomas Friedman, "Senseless in Israel," *New York Times*, November 24, 2000.

21. See Ali Abunimah and Hussein Ibish, "The U.S. Media and the New Intifada," in *The New Intifada*, ed. Roane Carey (New York: Verso Books, 2001), pp. 233–56.

22. Clayton Swisher, *The Truth about Camp David: The Untold Story about the Collapse of the Middle East Peace Process* (New York: Nation Books, 2004), pp. 226, 335–42.

23. Robert Malley, "Fictions about the failure at Camp David," *New York Times,* July 8, 2001. Along with Hussein Agha, Malley wrote a more comprehensive piece challenging the myth: "Camp David: the tragedy of errors," *New York Review of Books,* August 9, 2001.

24. Swisher, *Truth about Camp David,* p. x.

25. Ibid., pp. 206, 274.

26. Ibid., p. 206.

27. Ibid., pp. 318–19.

28. Ibid., p. 325.

29. Amos Oz, "Even if Camp David fails, this conflict is on its last legs," *Guardian,* July 25, 2000, cited in Yitzhak Laor, "The Tears of Zion," *New Left Review* (July–August 2001).

30. "Labor ready to relinquish East Jerusalem areas in peace deal," *Ha'aretz,* http://www.haaretzdaily.com/.

31. Yossi Beilin, *The Path to Geneva* (New York: RDV Books/Akashic Books, 2004), pp. 283–84.

32. Yossi Beilin and Yasser Abed Rabbo, "An accord to remember," *New York Times,* December 1, 2003.

33. Amram Mitzna, "They are afraid of peace," *Ha'aretz,* October 16, 2003.

34. http://www.geneva-accord.org (accessed June 3, 2005).

35. http://www.heskem.org.il/maps.asp (accessed June 3, 2005).

36. Beilin, *Path to Geneva,* pp. 261–62.

37. Frantz Fanon, "First Truths on the Colonial Problem," in *Toward the African Revolution* (New York: Grove Press, 1967), p. 122.

38. Beilin, p. 262.

39. Al Haq press release, "New position paper from Al-Haq: The Geneva Accord, a legal commentary," May 24, 2004.

40. Study by Tami Steinmetz Center for Peace Research at Tel Aviv University, cited in "The Peace Index: Israeli Jews fret over possibility of a binational state," *Ha'aretz,* November 5, 2003.

41. Howard Goller, Reuters, August 29, 2000; cited in Tanya Reinhart, *Israel/Palestine: How to End the War of 1948* (New York: Seven Stories Press, 2002), p. 40.

42. Larry Derfner, "Sounding the alarm about Israel's demographic crisis," *Forward,* January 9, 2004.

43. Yacov Ben Efrat, "A Misguided Conception," *Challenge* (January–February 2006).

44. Interview with Nahum Barnea, "Olmert parts from the territories," *Yedi'ot Aharonot Weekend Magazine,* December 5, 2003.

45. Ari Shavit, "An interview with Dov Weisglass, Sharon's lawyer," *Ha'aretz,* October 11, 2004.

46. Harvey Morris, "Israeli renouncement of Gaza not enough for Palestinians," *Financial Times,* September 13, 2005.

47. "Israel to expand security zone into northern Gaza," *Agence France Presse,* September 16, 2005.

48. "Israel will not allow Gaza port without control: minister," *Agence France Presse,* September 21, 2005.

49. Amira Hass, "Quartet envoy accuses Israel of foot-dragging over Gaza border," *Ha'aretz,* October 24, 2005.

50. For statistics on the number of days the crossing point was closed and information about food shortages, see "The Gaza Strip: February Access Report: Closure at Karni Crossing," Office of the Coordination of Humanitarian Affairs, March 8, 2006, http://www.humanitarianinfo.org/opt/docs/UN/OCHA/ochSR_Gaza Access_Feb06.pdf. For statements by UN officials, see Akiva Eldar, "UN aid workers: Gaza on verge of disaster," *Ha'aretz,* April 4, 2006. For details about shortages of medications caused by the closure see Press Release 32/2006: "IOF Re-close Karni Commercial Crossing and Impose a Siege on the Palestinian Civilian Population in the Gaza Strip," Palestinian Centre for Human Rights, April 6, 2006, available at http://pchrgaza.org/files/PressR/English/2006/37-2006.htm.

51. Aluf Benn, "Olmert: We must pull out from parts of West Bank," *Ha'aretz,* January 25, 2006, http://www.haaretzdaily.com.

52. Aluf Benn and Lilach Weissman, "Olmert: We must separate from the Palestinians," *Ha'aretz,* February 7, 2006.

53. "Not good enough," *Ha'aretz*, March 6, 2006.

54. Nahum Barnea, "Olmert parts from the territories," *Yedi'ot Aharonot Weekend Magazine*, December 5, 2003.

55. Ruthie Blum, "It's the Demography, Stupid." *Jerusalem Post*, May 20, 2004.

56. See, for example, "Israel vows 'zero tolerance' to Gaza violence," *Agence France Presse*, September 12, 2005.

57. "Creation of 'Death Zone' in northern Gaza Strip is illegal," *B'Tselem*, January 3, 2006, http://electronicintifada.net/v2/article4376. shtml.

58. Amos Harel, "Army escalates shelling of Gaza launch sites," *Ha'aretz*, April 7, 2006.

59. "Israeli raids fail to stem tide of Gaza rockets," *Agence France Presse*, April 7, 2006.

60. Daphna Golan-Agnon, *Next Year in Jerusalem* (New York: The New Press, 2005), p. 205.

3: IT COULD HAPPEN HERE

1. Orly Halpern, "Bauer: It could happen here," *Ha'aretz*, February 26, 2003.

2. At a meeting with American Jewish leaders in May 2005, Prime Minister Ariel Sharon stated that immigration was one of his government's key policy priorities, and it was his goal to bring one million immigrants to Israel in the next fifteen years. See Aluf Benn and Shlomo Shamir, "PM to U.S. Jewish leaders: I won't compromise on Jerusalem," *Ha'aretz*, May 23, 2005.

3. See William Montalbano, "Israel troubled by Soviet Jews' 'dropout' rate," *Los Angeles Times*, June 2, 1988.

4. Uri Schmetzer, "Israel tightens immigration rule; it's Jewish state or nowhere, exiting Soviets are told," *Chicago Tribune*, June 20, 1988.

5. See Dimitri Simes, "Locking Soviet Jews onto a one-way path; direct flights to Israel would deny émigrés their freedom of choice," *Los Angeles Times*, April 14, 1987; Robert Pear, "U.S. drafts plans to curb admission of Soviet Jews," *New York Times*, September 3, 1989.

6. Mazal Mualem and Aluf Benn, "Chief Rabbis call for revision to be made in Law of Return," *Ha'aretz*, August 25, 2002.

7. Central Bureau of Statistics (Israel), "Statistical Abstract of Israel 2004," Section 4.2, pp. 4–6.

8. According to Amos Hermon, chairman of the Jewish Agency Education Department, which cosponsors Masa with the Israeli government, the goal of the program is to increase Jewish immigration to Israel by providing youth with a year of "deep integration into Israeli society." In early 2006, according to Hermon, Masa and Birthright Israel were considering merging in order to strengthen their ability to contribute to the goal of bringing one million new immigrants. See Brianna Ames, "Birthright, MASA mull merger to boost participation; agency hopes joint program can bring million olim," *Jerusalem Post,* February 9, 2006. See also Aluf Benn and Shlomo Shamir, "PM to U.S. Jewish leaders: I won't compromise on Jerusalem," *Ha'aretz* Web site, May 23, 2005.

9. Figures from the "World Jewish Yearbook, 2002," available at the Web site of The Jewish Agency for Israel, http://www.jafi.org.il/ education/100/concepts/demography/demjpop.html (accessed May 23, 2005).

10. Michele Chabin, "Israel's bleak economy spurs reverse aliya—to U.S.," *Jewish News Weekly of Northern California,* August 29, 2003.

11. "2 in 3 FSU Jews opt for Germany over Israel," *Jerusalem Post,* December 3, 2004.

12. CIA World Factbook. See http://www.cia.gov/cia/publications/ factbook/fields/2112.html (accessed January 20, 2006).

13. Gideon Alon, "Number of returning Israelis continues to drop," *Ha'aretz,* November 19, 2003.

14. "EU passport gets popular in Israel," *Deutsche Welle,* July 21, 2004, available at http://www.dw-world.de/dw/article/0,,1273065,00 .html (accessed on May 17, 2005).

15. See, for example, Ellis Shuman, "Argentinian Jews flee economic instability for new lives in Israel," *IsraelInsider,* December 26, 2001, available at http://web.israelinsider.com/Articles/Politics/288 .htm (accessed May 18, 2005).

16. Central Bureau of Statistics (Israel), press release, "23,200 new immigrants arrived in Israel in 2003—31% less than in the previous year," January 25, 2004.

17. In January 2003, Rabbi Gabriel Farhi was stabbed outside his synagogue in rue Pétion in Paris. He claimed that he was attacked by a young, masked man who shouted "Allahu Akbar" ("God is Great!" in Arabic), prompting popular demonstrations against anti-Semitism. Inconsistencies in the rabbi's story led to a police investigation and allegations that the wounds, which were "superficial," were self-inflicted. Among the evidence police cited was the fact that the knife used in the attack had belonged to the synagogue's kitchen. (See Jean-Michel Décugis, Christophe Labbé, and Olivia Recasens, "Les mystères de l'affaire Farhi," *Le Point*, March 14, 2003.)

In July 2004, reports of a brutal anti-Semitic attack on a young woman on a train near Paris by Arab and African youths caused global outrage and provoked deep soul-searching and condemnation across France's political class, including from President Jacques Chirac. The story turned out to be a cruel hoax by a compulsive liar. Even after this became known, Prime Minister Ariel Sharon poured oil on the fire by claiming that the situation of French Jews had become so bad that they "must move to Israel" at once. (See *BBC*, "French Jews 'must move to Israel,'" July 18, 2004, available at http://news.bbc.co.uk/1/hi/world/middle_east/3904943.stm.) In August 2004, Israel's then foreign minister, Silvan Shalom, rushed to Paris following an arson attack at a Jewish community center in the city. After touring the gutted building, Shalom exclaimed, "I don't think any of us could believe that sixty years on, Jews would again live under a threat in Europe." Days later, French police arrested a disgruntled employee of the community center, a fifty-two-year-old mentally disturbed Jewish man, after finding in his home the markers used to draw swastikas on the walls of the center and other conclusive evidence that he had started the fire. (See "Israeli FM urges more action against anti-Semitism in France," *Agence France Presse*, August 24, 2004; and Olivia Recasens, Christophe Labbé, and Jean-Michel Décugis, "L'incendie du centre juif; Ce n'était qu'un fait divers," *Le Point*, September 2, 2004.)

18. Ellis Shuman, "Proposed campaign to promote aliya angers French Jews," *IsraelInsider*, June 14, 2004, available at http://web.israel insider.com/Articles/AntiSemi/3742.htm (accessed May 19, 2005).

19. Neri Livneh, "Coming Home," *Ha'aretz*, July 19, 2002.

20. Human Rights Watch, Amnesty International, International Commission of Jurists, joint statement, "Israeli discriminatory law tears apart thousands of families," May 24, 2005, available at http://electronicintifada.net/v2/article3873.shtml.

21. Hasan Jabarin, "From discrimination to denial of basic freedom," *Ha'aretz*, May 18, 2005.

22. Niv Hachlili, "The Boundaries of Love," *Ha'aretz*, March 24, 2006.

23. Aluf Benn and Yuval Yoaz, "PM backs temporary law enforcing tougher citizenship standards," *Ha'aretz*, April 4, 2005, http://www.haaretzdaily.com.

24. Yitzhak Kadman, "A more effective birth control," *Ha'aretz*, February 1, 2005.

25. In *Yediot Aharonot* in Hebrew: "Brigadier General (Res) Gazit: 'a dictatorship should be established here,'" March 26, 2001, available at http://www.ynet.co.il/articles/1,7340,L-623908,FF.html, trans. Dena Bugel-Shunra.

26. "Herzliya conference sees verbal attacks on Israeli Arabs," *Ha'aretz*, December 18, 2003.

27. Lily Galili, "Israeli-Russian journalist calls for castration as anti-terror step," *Ha'aretz*, January 28, 2002.

28. Article II(d) and Article III(c). See http://preventgenocide.org.

29. Jewish People Policy Planning Institute, *Annual Assessment 2005* (Jerusalem: JPPI, July 2005), pp. 14–16.

30. "Israeli citizenship for $1,000 and basic training," *Ha'aretz*, July 11, 2005, http://www.haaretzdaily.com.

31. Nur Masalha, *Expulsion of the Palestinians: The Concept of 'Transfer' in Zionist Political Thought 1882–1948* (Washington, DC: Institute for Palestine Studies, 1992).

32. Nur Masalha, *An Israeli Plan to Transfer Galilee's Christians to South*

America: Yosef Weitz and Operation Yohanan, CMEIS Occasional Paper No. 55 (Durham, UK: University of Durham, Centre for Middle Eastern and Islamic Studies, August 1996).

33. Ari Shavit, "Survival of the fittest," *Ha'aretz,* September 1, 2004.

34. See http://www.moledet.org.il/english (accessed May 20, 2005).

35. Sandro Contenta, "Hawk tries to build a nest in cabinet," *Toronto Star,* March 4, 2001.

36. See Khaled Amayreh, "New party calls for expulsion of non-Jews," Aljazeera.net, September 12, 2004, http://english.aljazeera.net/NR/exeres/3DBAEF08-AB3D-484B-AE66-740BC803DE57.htm; and "National Jewish Front calls for expelling Arabs from Israel," IsraelNationalNews.com, September 10, 2004, http://www.israelnn.com/news.php3?id=68762.

37. Boris Shusteff, "The logistics of transfer," July 3, 2002, available at http://www.gamla.org.il/english/article/2002/july/b1.htm (accessed May 22, 2005).

38. Tom Segev, "A black flag hangs over the idea of transfer," *Ha'aretz,* April 5, 2002.

39. I spoke with Foxman and the AIPAC representative Rebecca Needler when researching an article, "AIPAC, ADL refuse to condemn inclusion of ethnic cleansers in new Israel government," which was published in the *Daily Star* (Beirut) on March 3, 2003, and is available at http://electronicintifada.net/v2/article1210.shtml.

40. Foxman said he had not read the relevant party platforms "in a while," a remarkable admission from a man whose organization apparently scrutinizes for evidence of anti-Semitism almost every obscure pamphlet issued in the backstreets of Cairo. "I will go back and read them," Foxman assured, "and if transfer becomes part of the coalition agreement, then you can be sure you will hear from us." No statement was ever issued, and even today a search for "Moledet" on the ADL's Web site yields no result. Following the 2006 Israeli election, the ADL issued several statements about the results, none of which mentioned the extremist positions espoused by several of the parties.

41. The National Union solicits for financial contributions in the

United States through an organization called American Friends of Israel's National Union, which explicitly states "that the primary danger to the physical existence of the State [of Israel] is its demographics," and that the only solution to the conundrum is the immediate "repatriation" of Palestinians to "Arab lands." See http://www.thenationalunion.com/AFINU/survival .html (accessed May 20, 2005).

42. In interview with the *Jerusalem Post*'s Caroline Glick, "Sharon's accidental tourist," July 11, 2003.

43. *Congressional Record, U.S. Senate*, March 4, 2002, p. S1427.

44. Ali Abunimah, Nigel Parry, and Laurie King-Irani, "Republican Party leader calls for ethnic cleansing of Palestinians on prime time talk show," the Electronic Intifada, May 2, 2002, available at http://www.electronicintifada.net/v2/article569.shtml.

45. *Jerusalem Post*, July 11, 2003.

46. Amnon Barzilai, "More Israeli Jews favor transfer of Palestinians, Israeli Arabs, poll finds," *Ha'aretz*, March 12, 2002.

47. Yoav Stern, "Poll. Most Israeli Jews say Arabs should emigrate," *Ha'aretz*, April 4, 2005.

4: A UNITED, DEMOCRATIC STATE IN PALESTINE-ISRAEL

1. Martin Buber, *A Land of Two Peoples: Martin Buber on Jews and Arabs*, ed. Paul Mendes-Flohr (New York: Oxford University Press, 1983), p. 223.

2. See Judah Magnes et al., *Palestine—Divided or United?* (Jerusalem: Achva Cooperative Printing Press, 1947; repr., Westport, CT: Greenwood Press, 1983).

3. Buber, *Land of Two Peoples*, p. 199.

4. Ibid., p. 74.

5. *Washington Post*, June 16, 1969.

6. Alain Gresh, *The PLO: The Struggle Within* (London: Zed Books, 1988), p. 33.

7. Ibid., p. 45.

8. Descriptions and analyses of the varieties of federalism adopted by countries around the world can be found in a series of volumes published by the Forum on Federalisms. A good starting point is this comparative study of twelve federal states: John Kincaid and Alan Tarr (eds.), *Constitutional Origins, Structure, and Change in Federal Countries* (Montreal: McGill–Queen's University Press, 2005).

9. Mazal Mualem, "Census: Arabs form largest constituency in Labor Party," *Ha'aretz*, June 3, 2005.

10. For a history and analysis of the impact of Belgium's constitutional development on ethnic conflict in the country, see Liesbet Hooghe, "Belgium: Hollowing the Center," in *Federalism and Territorial Cleavages*, ed. Ugo Amoretti and Nancy Bermeo (Baltimore: Johns Hopkins University Press, 2004), pp. 55–93.

11. Felice Dassetto, "Belgique, België, '.be,'" *La Libre Belgique*, February 5, 2006, my translation from French.

12. As the linguistic conflict increasingly took on a territorial aspect, Belgium "irrevocably" fixed the frontiers between the linguistic regions in the 1960s; however, some disputes remain. The struggle over whether Voeren/Fourons—a municipality of six villages with about five thousand inhabitants, assigned to the Flemish region—should remain where it is or be moved to the Walloon region occasionally resulted in violence in the 1970s and 1980s. Though this has abated, the issue remains contentious. The status of six communes on the outskirts of Brussels that are included in the Flemish region is also hotly contested by Walloon nationalists; attaching the communes to the Walloon region would fulfill a key goal of Walloon separatists of creating contiguity between the Walloon region and Brussels. Although there is broad agreement on the fixed regional frontiers and little territorial conflict, this consensus would be unlikely to survive a serious attempt by any region to secede from Belgium. In this sense, Belgium, despite the claims of Flemish and Walloon separatists, is probably unpartitionable. Indeed, for more than a century, the decisions of Flemish and Walloon leaders demonstrated an understanding that the only thing worse than trying to get their communities to live together in a single state would be the attempt to divide the country.

13. Meron Benvenisti, "The key word is 'bizonal,'" *Ha'aretz*, February 26, 2004.

14. A caveat is that although the community governments are nonterritorial, French speakers living in Flanders cannot vote for the French community government. The "community" is defined for purposes of electing its government as being French speakers in the Walloon region and French speakers in the Brussels region. The converse is true for the Flemish community government. Additionally, the Flemish community and Flanders regions decided as a practical matter to merge their parliaments, although constitutionally these are distinct and could be separated. The French community government maintains a separate structure from the Walloon region.

15. For a detailed discussion of the legal aspects of the right of return, and a consideration of the principal arguments offered for and against it, see Ali Abunimah and Hussein Ibish, *The Palestinian Right of Return* (Washington, DC: ADC, 2001).

16. Salman Abu-Sitta in interview with Laila El-Haddad, "Palestinian right of return is feasible," Al Jazeera, May 21, 2005, available at http://electronicintifada.net/v2/article3894.shtml.

17. See Salman Abu-Sitta, "From Refugees to Citizens at Home" (London: Palestine Land Society, 2001).

18. Abu-Sitta, 2001, http://www.plands.org/books/citizen/The_Logistics_of_Return.htm.

19. For a comprehensive study, see Majid al-Haj, *Education, Empowerment and Control: The Case of the Arabs in Israel* (Albany: State University of New York Press, 1995).

20. See Human Rights Watch press release, "Israel Budget Discriminates Against Arab Citizens," August 12, 2004, http://hrw.org/english/docs/2004/08/12/isrlpa9228.htm, and full-length study, "Second Class: Discrimination Against Palestinian Arab Children in Israel's Schools," Human Rights Watch, 2001, http://www.hrw.org/reports/2001/israel2. For a detailed account of funding disparities and other structural inequalities, see Zama Coursen-Neff, "Discrimination Against Palestinian Arab children in the Israeli Educational System," *Journal of International Law and Politics* 36 (2004), pp. 749–1032.

21. Cited in Daphna Golan-Agnon, *Next Year in Jerusalem* (New York: The New Press, 2005), p. 178.

22. "UNRWA Medium Term Plan, 2005–2009" (Gaza: UNRWA, 2005), p. 19.

23. Nathan Brown, *Democracy, History and the Contest over the Palestinian Curriculum* (Adam Institute, 2001), available at http://www.geocities.com/nathanbrown1/Adam_Institute_Palestinian_textbooks.htm (accessed August 31, 2005).

24. See "Analysis and Evaluation of the New Palestinian Curriculum: Reviewing Palestinian Textbooks and Tolerance Education Program" (Jerusalem: IPCRI, March 2003); and "Analysis and Evaluation of the New Palestinian Curriculum: Reviewing Palestinian Textbooks and Tolerance Education Program Grades 4 & 9" (Jerusalem: IPCRI, June 2004).

25. Cited in Palestinian Ministry of Education, "The Myth of Incitement in Palestinian Textbooks," June 8, 2005, available at http://www.pcdc.edu.ps/Myth_of_Palestinian_textbook_incitement.pdf.

26. See http://www.handinhandk12.org for more information.

27. Yigal Bronner. Interviewed in Chicago, April 4, 2006.

28. See Claire McGlynn, Ulrike Niens, Ed Cairns, and Miles Hewstone, "Moving Out of Conflict: The Contribution of Integrated Schools in Nothern Ireland to Identity, Attitudes, Forgiveness and Reconciliation," *Journal of Peace Education* 1, no. 2 (September 2004); and Claire McGlynn, "Integrated Education in Northern Ireland in the Context of Critical Multiculturalism," *Irish Educational Studies* 22, no. 3 (Winter 2003).

5: LEARNING FROM SOUTH AFRICA

1. F. W. de Klerk, *The Last Trek* (London: Pan Books, 1999), p. xix.

2. On December 3, 2002, Students for Peaceful Coexistence and the Global Voices Program at the University of Chicago hosted a panel on the "Differences Between Criticism of Israel and Anti-Semitism." The panelists were Ali Abunimah, Peter Novick, Arnold Wolf, and Emily Hauser. A transcript of the remarks of each panelist is at http://electronicintifada.net/v2/article975.shtml.

3. Anthony Sampson, *Mandela* (New York: Knopf, 1999), p. 520.

4. "South Africa reaches out to Israeli 'friends,'" *Agence France Presse*, September 7, 2004.

5. Nelson Mandela, *Long Walk to Freedom* (New York: Little, Brown, 1995; first paperback edition), p. 124.

6. De Klerk, *Last Trek*, p. 6.

7. Mandela, *Long Walk to Freedom*, p. 111.

8. See Donald Akenson, *God's Peoples: Covenant and Land in South Africa, Israel, and Ulster* (Ithaca, NY: Cornell University Press, 1992).

9. Oren Yiftachel, "Ending the colonialism," *Ha'aretz*, July 19, 2005.

10. Speech delivered by Dave Steward on behalf of former president F. W. de Klerk to the Institut Choiseul, Paris, June 14, 2004, available at http://www.fwdklerk.org.za/download_speech/04_06_14_D WS_Institut_Choiseul_S.doc.

11. The central argument of Tom Segev's history of the Mandate period, *One Palestine, Complete* (New York: Metropolitan Books, 2000), is to demonstrate the reliance of the Zionist movement on British power, and Britain's structural and political partiality to the movement's advancement.

12. Mandela, *Long Walk to Freedom*, p. 179.

13. *Ha'aretz*, April 4, 1969, cited in David Hirst, *The Gun and the Olive Branch* (New York: Nation Books, 2003), p. 221.

14. See "The growing trade links with South Africa," *Business Week*, May 22, 1978; and "South Africa and Israel: an alliance of pragmatism," *Christian Science Monitor*, September 25, 1985.

15. Benjamin Beit-Hallahmi, *The Israeli Connection: Who Israel Arms and Why* (New York: Pantheon Books, 1987).

16. See ibid., pp. 129–36; and Claire Hoy and Victor Ostrovsky, *By Way of Deception* (Toronto: Stoddart, 1990), p. 151.

17. Meron Benvenisti, *Conflicts and Contradictions* (New York: Villard Books, 1986), p. 112.

18. De Klerk, *Last Trek*, p. 15.

19. Ibid., p. 16.

20. Ibid., p. 393.

21. Ibid., p. 40.

22. Speaking on BBC 2's *Newsnight*, cited by Daphna Baram in "Disengagement and ethnic cleansing," *Guardian*, August 16, 2005.

23. Eelco van der Linden, "Een 'baie' gelukkige oer-Afrikaner," *Haagsche Courant*, October 16, 2004, translation from Dutch by Mouin Rabbani.

24. Aviva Lori, "Now it's your turn," *Ha'aretz*, May 16, 2003.

25. De Klerk, *Last Trek*, p. 30.

26. Mandela, *Long Walk to Freedom*, p. 483.

27. De Klerk, *Last Trek*, p. 106.

28. Speech delivered by Dave Steward on behalf of former president F. W. de Klerk to the Institut Choiseul, Paris, June 14, 2004. Full text available from the FW de Klerk Foundation, http://www.fwdklerk.org.za.

29. Ibid.

30. Mahmoud Mamdani, *Good Muslim, Bad Muslim: America, the Cold War, and the Roots of Terror* (New York: Pantheon Books, 2004), p. 227.

31. Ibid., p. 228.

32. Mandela, *Long Walk to Freedom*, p. 177.

33. Mamdani, *Good Muslim, Bad Muslim*, p. 228.

34. See Azmi Bishara, "4 May 1999 and Palestinian Statehood: To Declare or Not to Declare," *Journal of Palestine Studies* 28, no. 2, pp. 5–16; and Joseph Massad, *The Persistence of the Palestinian Question* (New York: Routledge, 2006), pp. 143–53.

35. See Pierre Hugo, "Towards Darkness and Death: Racial Demonology in South Africa," *Journal of Modern African Studies* 26, no. 4 (1988), pp. 567–90.

36. Sampson, *Mandela*, p. 513.

37. Mandela, *Long Walk to Freedom*, p. 539.

38. Sampson, *Mandela*, p. 405.

39. See, for example, Jonathan Hyslop, "Problems of Explanation in the Study of Afrikaner Nationalism: A Case Study of the West Rand," *Journal of Southern African Studies* 22, no. 3 (September 1996).

40. Sampson, *Mandela*, p. 450.

41. De Klerk, *Last Trek*, p. 124.

42. Sampson, *Mandela*, p. 520.

43. Mandela, *Long Walk to Freedom*, p. 520.

44. Ibid., p. 283.

45. Ibid., p. 273.

46. Ibid., p. 537.

47. Joel Greenberg, "For many in Arab town, Israelis 'should feel what we feel,'" *New York Times,* April 8, 1994.

48. See polls conducted by the Palestinian Center for Policy and Survey Research at http://www.pcpsr.org/survey/cprspolls/index.html.

49. Mamdani, *Good Muslim, Bad Muslim*, p. 226.

50. Ibid.

51. "Tonge sacked over suicide comment," BBC News, January 23, 2004, available at http://news.bbc.co.uk/1/hi/uk_politics/3421669.stm.

52. Mamdani, *Good Muslim, Bad Muslim*, p. 227.

53. Ibid.

54. Aviva Lori, "Now it's your turn," *Ha'aretz*, May 16, 2003.

55. The Institute for Justice and Reconciliation (IJR) in Cape Town publishes regular surveys and research reports on public attitudes in South Africa. In addition to gathering data to monitor the actual situation, the IJR has also developed a wealth of knowledge about what reconciliation means and what promotes it in practice. See http://www.ijr.org.za.

56. Interview on *Democracy Now!* with Amy Goodman, February 23, 2006. Transcript available at http://www.democracynow.org/article .pl?sid=06/02/23/1454239.

57. *Ubuntu* is a word in the Zulu and Xhosa languages of South Africa describing a concept of humanity that is hard to render directly into English. Archbishop Desmond Tutu has said, "A person with ubuntu is open and available to others, affirming of others, does not feel threatened that others are able and good, for he or she has a proper self-assurance that comes from knowing that he or she belongs in a greater whole and is diminished when others are humiliated or diminished, when others are tortured or oppressed" (Desmond Tutu, *No Future Without Forgiveness* [New York: Image Books, 2000], p. 31).

6: ISRAELIS AND PALESTINIANS THINKING THE UNTHINKABLE

1. Michael Tarazi, "Two peoples, one state," *New York Times*, October 4, 2004.

2. Interview with Michael Tarazi in Ramallah, occupied West Bank, via telephone, September 16, 2005.

3. Peter Hirschberg, "Hello, I'm Israeli-Palestinian," *Inter Press Service*, February 10, 2004.

4. All the polls of the JMCC are available at its Web site, http://www.jmcc.org; see, for example, JMCC Public Opinion Poll No. 44, March 2002, and JMCC Public Opinion Poll No. 44, May 2005.

5. Amira Hass, lecture, Barnard College, April 11, 2005.

6. Interview with Khaled Amayreh in Hebron, occupied West Bank, via e-mail, July 23, 2005.

7. "Despite Hamas win, Palestinians want peace with Israel," *Agence France Presse*, January 30, 2006.

8. Khaled Meshal, "We will not sell our people or principles for foreign aid," *Guardian*, January 31, 2006.

9. "Hamas 'ready to talk to Israel,'" BBC News Online, February 8, 2006.

10. "Palestinian recognition of Israel a mistake, Hamas says," Reuters, February 6, 2006.

11. Mousa Abu Marzook, "What Hamas is seeking," *Washington Post*, January 31, 2006.

12. Shaul Mishal and Avraham Sela, *The Palestinian Hamas: Vision, Violence, and Coexistence* (New York: Columbia University Press, 2000), p. viii.

13. "Israeli Jews see Hamas as existential threat: poll," *Agence France Presse*, February 7, 2006.

14. See David Hirst, "Rush to annexation: Israel in Jerusalem," *Journal of Palestine Studies* 3, no. 4 (1974), pp. 3–31.

15. Ian Fisher, "Tens of thousands protest cartoon in Gaza," *New York Times*, February 3, 2006.

16. Khalil Shikaki, "The Polls: What the Palestinians really voted for," *Newsweek*, February 6, 2006.

17. Adam Hanieh, "The end of a political fiction?" Electronic Intifada, February 2, 2006.

18. Edward Said, "Bases of Coexistence," *Al-Hayat*, November 1997 (reprinted in Edward Said, *The End of the Peace Process: Oslo and After* [New York: Vintage Books, 2001], ch. 31, pp. 205–9).

19. See Ghada Karmi, "A secular democratic state in historic Palestine: An idea whose time has come?" *Al-Adab* (Beirut), July 2002; George Bisharat, "Two-state solution again sells Palestinians short," *Los Angeles Times*, January 25, 2004; and the book by Mazin Qumsiyeh, *Sharing the Land of Canaan* (London: Pluto Press, 2004).

20. Meron Benvenisti, "Which kind of binational state?" *Ha'aretz*, November 20, 2003.

21. Daniel Gavron, *The Other Side of Despair: Jews and Arabs in the Promised Land* (Lanham, MD: Rowman and Littlefield, 2004), p. 224.

22. Ibid., p. 229.

23. Peter Hirschberg, "One-state awakening," *Haaretz*, December 12, 2004.

24. Gavron, *Other Side of Despair*, pp. 178–79.

25. Yoram Binur, *My Enemy, My Self* (New York: Doubleday, 1989).

26. George Hishmeh, "Actions speak louder than words," *Jordan Times*, May 13, 2005.

27. Personal interview, September 6, 2005, by telephone.

28. Personal interview, September 8, 2005, Michigan City, Indiana.

29. The "Olga Document" was distributed widely over the Internet. A copy can be found at http://electronicintifada.net/bytopic/historicaldocuments/285.shtml.

30. See http://www.pacbi.org.

31. Chester Crocker, *High Noon in Southern Africa: Making Peace in a Rough Neighborhood*, cited in Anthony Sampson, *Mandela* (New York: Knopf, 1999), p. 316.

32. "Church of England votes to divest from Caterpillar," Electronic Intifada, February 6, 2006, available at http://electronicintifada.net/v2/article4468.shtml.

33. Oliver Duff, Rob Sharp, and Eric Silver, "Architects threaten to boycott Israel over 'apartheid' barrier," *Independent*, February 10, 2006.

34. See Coalition Against Israeli Apartheid press release, "CUPE Ontario votes in Support of Boycott, Divestment, Sanctions Against

Israeli Apartheid," May 29, 2006, http://electronicintifada.net /v2/article4745.shtml; and PACBI press release, "Palestinians welcome UK vote for Israel academic boycott," May 29, 2006, http://elctronicintifada.net/v2/article4743.shtml.

35. Abraham Foxman, "Blurring the line," *Ha'aretz*, April 5, 2004.

36. Laurie Goodstein, "Threat to divest is church tool in Israeli fight," *New York Times*, August 6, 2005.

37. "Norwegian minister apologizes for call to boycott Israeli brands," *Ha'aretz*, January 7, 2006.

38. Tamara Traubman, "U.S. Jews block conference in which anti-Israel professors participating," *Ha'aretz*, February 10, 2006.

39. "Foreign Ministry warns Israel, Europe on collision course," *Ha'aretz*, October 13, 2004.

40. The Israeli Committee Against House Demolitions was the first Israeli peace group to call for sanctions against Israel. See "ICAHD first Israeli peace group to call for sanctions," January 27, 2005, available at http://www.icahd.org/eng/news.asp?menu=5&sub menu=1&item=218.

41. Thomas Friedman, "One wall, one person, one vote," *New York Times*, September 14, 2003.

ACKNOWLEDGMENTS

All writers have moments when they feel they've lost perspective, which is when they must be able to rely on someone whose judgment they trust absolutely. I have been extremely fortunate to have several such people in my life. This book would not exist without Riva Hocherman, my editor at Metropolitan Books, whose wise guidance, insight, faith in it, and red pencil have been essential at every stage. All the staff at Metropolitan Books, and especially Sara Bershtel, have given invaluable help and support. I am indebted to Joseph Massad for his close reading of the manuscript and his comments, which helped strengthen my arguments, and to David Boodell who was generous with his time at crucial moments, dramatically improving the clarity and style of several sections. Anthony Arnove, my agent, deserves particular thanks for his outstanding work, and for persuading me that a book was worth writing. I am grateful for the love, friendship, and support given to me by Benjamin Doherty; I could never have done without him.

The ideas expressed here have developed over several years in the course of many discussions with family, friends, and colleagues too numerous to list in full. The most important of these is my father. From the earliest age, his memories of Palestine, like my mother's, allowed me to feel that I belonged to a country I never had a chance to see until my twenty-fifth year. But he also taught me never to turn that love into a tribal impulse and always to see the condition of Palestinians as one connected to universal human struggles. His life's work taught me two other lessons that I hope are embodied in this book: always seek dialogue and understanding with those who have wronged you but never waver from the pursuit of justice and fairness.

I would like also to mention Jennifer Bing-Canar, Michael Brown, Lousie Cainkar, Charity Crouse, Hussein Ibish, and Dawne Moon. I often replayed our many conversations as I set my arguments down on paper. I thank Professor Eugene Rogan at St. Antony's College, Oxford. His invitation to me to present a lecture as part of a seminar titled "Palestinians on Palestine" in early 2004 spurred me to write the paper that formed the core of this project.

The inspirational efforts of the Chicago Palestine Film Festival over several years allowed me to see films that I would not have had access to otherwise. The perspectives I gained directly enriched my thinking and influenced my work. I have been privileged to be part of the Electronic Intifada team. Nigel Parry, Laurie King, Arjan El Fassed, Maureen Clare Murphy, Ken Harper, and all those whose contributions have made the Web site what it is are my heroes.

I would like to thank Harold Richman and Michael Little for their personal support, and Jason Nakhleh, for his heroic efforts. I should add that while I am grateful to all those individuals and organizations, my acknowledging them in no way implies that they endorse my views.

My family has played an important part in inspiring me to write this book. The beautiful jacket designed by my sister Ruba literally wraps it in the unqualified love and support I have felt from her, from my mother, Samira, my father, Hasan, and Henry, Yasmin, Henry Hasan, Maye, Jonathan, and Layla.

INDEX

ABOUT THE AUTHOR

ALI ABUNIMAH, a Palestinian-American, is the cocreator and an editor of the Electronic Intifada Web site, since 2001, and more recently of Electronic Iraq and Electronic Lebanon. A graduate of Princeton University and the University of Chicago, he has written for the *Chicago Tribune,* among other publications. A resident of Chicago, he also directs research for the design of children's services in the United States and Europe.